PRAISE FOR MICHAEL PATRICK WELCH

"I've been friends with Michael Patrick Welch for a number of years, and in New Orleans he seems to have really found his place. On my first visit from New York, before the flood, he took me on an epic bike ride tour of the city. We saw everything from grand mansions to beautiful bombed-out neighborhoods, and no matter where we went that day, Michael knew someone. Michael obviously loves New Orleans very much, and on my visits there, he has shown me so much that I never expected, and would have not seen otherwise."

—Jonathan Ames, creator of HBO's *Bored to Death*, and author of *The Extra Man* and *The Double Life Is Twice As Good*.

"Your boyfriend is very, very talented."

—Ray Davies of The Kinks to Michael Patrick Welch's girlfriend, at JazzFest 2003.

New Orleans

The Underground Guide

Michael Patrick Welch

With Photos by

Zack Smith &
Jonathan Traviesa

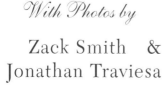

ISBN: 978-1-60801-079-0

Copyright © 2011 UNO Press

2nd Edition (October 2011)

University of New Orleans Press

Managing Editor, Bill Lavender

unopress.org

ACKNOWLEDGEMENTS

We would first like to acknowledge that any attempt to comprehensively document every one of New Orleans' music and art communities would be impossible. Further editions of this book will fill in any embarrassing holes we may have left this first time around.

Writing by **Michael Patrick Welch**, *with* **Alison Fensterstock**.

Photos by **Zack Smith** *and* **Jonathan Traviesa**.

Book Design by **Creighton Durrant**

Back cover photo of Ratty Scurvics et al donated by **Shannon Brinkman**.

Maps by **Morgana King**.

Other photo contributors: **Aubrey Edwards, Dan Fox, Robin Walker, Alleyn Evans, Taslim Van Huttum, Rachel Breunlin, Eduard Keller, Scott Stuntz, Tamara Grayson, Rafael Forest, Paul Grass, J. Lloyd Miller, Black Sails Photography, Kim Welsh,** *and* **Morgana King**.

Other writing contributors: **Andrei Codrescu, Dan Fox, Renard "Slangston Hughes" Bridgewater, Daniel "Impulss" Perez, Leo McGovern,** *and* **Jack Porobil**.

Special thanks to **Dan Fox, Creighton Durrant** *and also* **Juvenile, Andrei Codrescu, Dr. Ike Padnos, Geoff Douville, Otis Fenell, Gambit Weekly,** *and* **Anti-Gravity Magazine**.

CONTENTS

WELCOME TO NEW ORLEANS!

It's Not What You Think!

We wrote *New Orleans: The Underground Guide* to counter the false image of New Orleans that you have in your head. It's not your fault; someone put it there. New Orleans is marketed, largely from within, as its old self. Sure New Orleans still sounds like brass bands, Mardi Gras Indians and trad-jazz. But New Orleans' old-school image has been a marketing template the tourist industry is loathe to relinquish. New Orleans is marketed as if The French Quarter is still bursting with culture, when really it has turned into a beautiful shopping mall where almost none of the city's important modern day music is made, or even played (Bourbon Street in particular is more than happy to accommodate your outdated notions of the city). New Orleans' past should be glorified, its amazing traditions kept alive, but not if it means the world ends up thinking New Orleans' most important artistic days are behind us! There are things happening here, now, that in fact *are in the process* of changing the way the world views music and art – again, as New Orleans always has.

We made this music-focused guidebook partly to prove that new millennium New Orleans sounds pretty damned different. New Orleans' artistic communities are still as unique and vibrant, and conjure up as many important new creations as ever. We made *New Orleans: The Underground Guide* for tourists who don't want New Orleans marketed to them. You want natural adventures! And though all guidebooks purport to be street-level accounts of where the locals hang out – well, we've each lived in New Orleans for many years, participating wholeheartedly in its music, art, journalism, publishing, even burlesque scenes, and when we scribbled down hundred of places where we regularly go hang-out and see music and art, few of our awesome, historic, truly popular, New Orleans-culture-defining choices could be found in almost any other guidebook.

As you see, something needed to be done.

And we figured that the best thing we could do would be to act as friends of yours who live here, who want you to meet our wild, artistic friends and to truly understand how much fun we have, and why we love living here. And that reason, mainly, is music. Even our extensive FOOD section features, almost exclusively, eating spots that also host live music.

As for how to read our guidebook, we hoped that *New Orleans: The Underground Guide* would be somewhat enjoyable to read – even for a local – all the way from start to finish. Within the listings we stop and tell little informative anecdotes – called N.O. Moments – about the New Orleans places and people we like best: Romanian transplant/author **Andrei Codrescu** writes about New Orleans places best suited for thoughtful bohemian productive relaxation, while rapper **Juvenile** suggests where not to go in New Orleans if you ain't got a gun. If you don't want to read the book like a novel, at least consider reading from start to finish the MUSICIANS section, wherein we describe over 100 of New Orleans best modern, non-traditional bands, solo-artists, rappers and DJs – musicians who sound like New Orleans, without playing old New Orleans music.

We've practiced this same ideology with all our choices here, hoping to prove, to you, that New Orleans is not what you think.

– *Michael Patrick Welch*

JT

The bike rack outside Pal's Lounge, Mid-City, has more than one use.

SEVEN AWESOME NEIGHBORHOODS

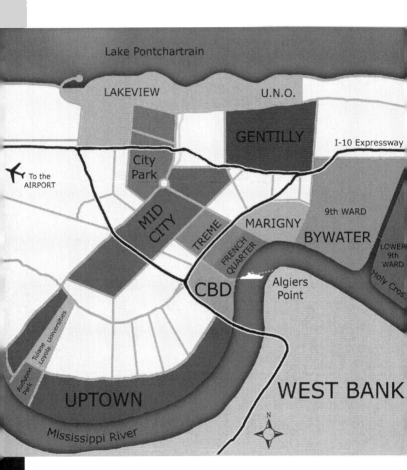

As a visitor, you will understand and enjoy New Orleans more if you think in terms of neighborhoods. Many of New Orleans' neighborhoods were creamed by floodwaters; 'hoods that tourists rarely visited. Which is why, now, visitors who stick solely to the longtime tourist meccas of the French Quarter or Garden District (which were both almost entirely undamaged) often leave thinking everything's fine.

This book admittedly overlooks many New Orleans neighborhoods that were wiped out and are slowly rebuilding, opting instead to help you explore the surviving heart of the city, which is also the most easily traversable. It should be noted, though, that New Orleans' furthest reaches and suburbs and still-struggling areas all possess their own charms – the still-thriving Vietnamese community in flood-ravaged New Orleans East (see *Food*) is one great example. The 'burbs also often, not incidentally, feature some of the best locals'-favorite restaurants, from seafood on the Lakefront to Italian in Kenner. But for our purposes, we'll skip the burbs for the most part and stick to the basics – downtown (*Marigny/ Bywater*) and its most immediate walkable, bikable, public transport-accessible environs.

Also, when we refer to "neighborhoods," we almost never mean the French Quarter. The Quarter is technically a neighborhood too (which is why the city fines bars and restaurants that host unregulated live music. Can you believe that?), but nowadays the Quarter is mostly a very beautiful mall that caters/panders to tourists. It has its cool little secrets and stalwart holdouts, as well as historical curiosities (that Laundromat on Rampart was once **Cosimo Matassa's** legendary recording studio) but we're here to make sure you spend time exploring New Orleans' "real" neighborhoods, enjoying good conversation and adventures with the many friendly, interesting, artistic locals you wont meet on Bourbon Street (unless they're bussing your table, or giving you a lap dance).

We will address these seven 'hoods as they are connected, one to the next, starting in the east and moving downriver, west: 1) **Bywater**, 2) **Faubourg Marigny**, 3) **French Quarter**, 4) **Central Business District (CBD)**, 5) **Uptown**. Then North of the Quarter there's... 6) **Faubourg Tremé**, 7) **Mid City**.

BYWATER

Boundaries: Florida Ave. (north), Mississippi River (south), Industrial Canal and levee (east), Press St. railroad tracks (west).

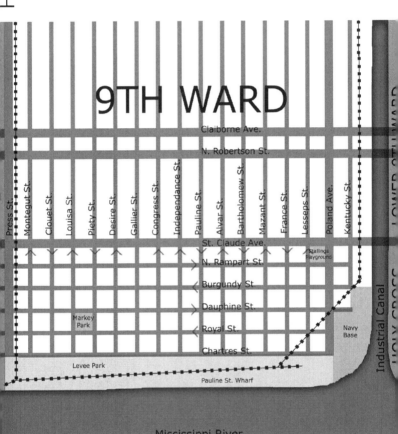

The way most guidebooks focus on the French Quarter, we will harp on Bywater (and its sister neighborhood, Marigny). Bywater's art and music scene are as close as New Orleans comes to "hip," though rarely pretentious. Many locals claim that, long ago, real estate agents coined the term Bywater (meaning, by both the river and the industrial canal, which separates it from the infamous Lower Nine) to disassociate the area from the rest of the Ninth Ward. But especially since the neighborhood totally survived Katrina, the rents for Bywater's many big, classic, hundred-year-old shotgun houses have gone up. Developers talk of a giant cruise terminal in the 'hood, and luxury loft spaces. But the neighborhood's dense community of artists and musicians have deep roots here, and it will be a while before they're forced out. Until then, Bywater is one of America's last true bohemian paradises.

For now the neighborhood is pleasantly mixed: a house flipper's dream stands freshly painted between dilapidated beauties that more-or-less poor residents ain't giving up any time soon (thank god), since they're right down the street from the world's greatest bars. Bywater is still down-low enough that residents host random music festivals without any noise complaints, while the guy up the street plans his secret speakeasy after-party. If you came to New Orleans for true gritty, funky art and fun, and if you came to follow strange locals on adventures often involving bikes and beer and pot and music, then Bywater. Bywater.

ZS

FAUBOURG MARIGNY

(FAW-BORG MER-IH-NEE)

Boundaries: St. Claude Ave. (north), Mississippi River
(south), Franklin Ave. (east), Esplanade Ave. (west)

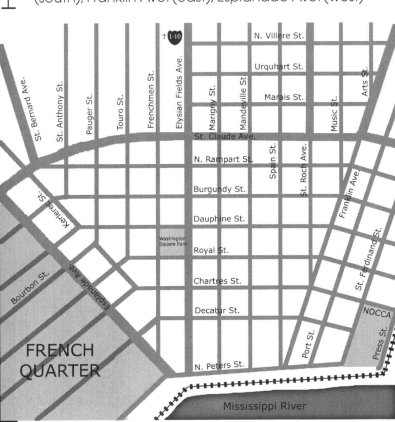

The Faubourg Marigny is cleaner, more expensive, and more charmingly crammed together than Bywater, but everyone from all over the city plays and hears music on Frenchmen Street and in other down-low neighborhood venues. The Marigny is half entertainment district (the locals' mellow Bourbon St.) and the other half residential streets of small, yardless 19th century Creole cottages in pastels and pinks and yellows and blues. The residents do have money (lots of good-looking gay folks in the Marigny), but they can't really be considered snobs, choosing to live and participate in one of the wilder, weirder parts of town. Don't be lulled, though, by the smell of high rents; muggers are drawn to that smell too. Keep your wits about you, remain on your bike, look around, stay alert, and move with friends whenever possible.

THE FRENCH QUARTER

Boundaries: Pretty much a big lopsided square, bordered by Rampart St. (north,) Decatur St. (south), Esplanade Ave. (east), and Canal St. (west)

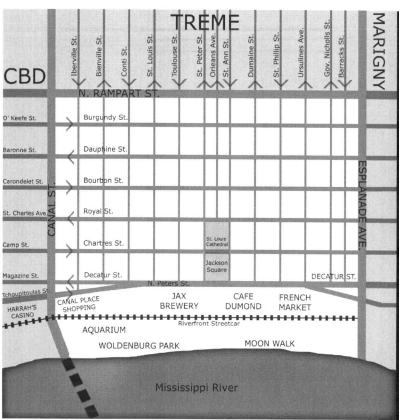

The French Quarter is still (somewhat) a functioning mixed-use residential/commercial neighborhood. It's also a giant open-air mall of bars, antique shopping, street performers, more bars, bad art, strip clubs, daiquiri stands and, in its margins, old-timey New Orleans music. Even if the Quarter isn't overrated, it's definitely overexposed, considering so many tourists spend their whole vacations there, in the mall, neglecting all other New Orleans exploration. It's a fun section of town, but the only locals you'll likely meet are your waiter or bartender. Even many of the strippers come from out of town for our local holidays.

It is, though, utterly beautiful, and perfect for endless wandering and stumbling. Every other block or so, you'll discover a place like **The Chart Room** *(300 Chartres St.),* which allows for amazing people-watching, and charges just $2.50 for any well drink. **Jackson Square** hosts tarot readers, "psychics," questionable artists hawking their wares and gold-painted statue people, all to the tune of good brass bands (many of the city's best traditional players hone their chops in the Square, passing the hat) and bad folk music. There's also the old **French Market** on Lower Decatur (near the river just off Esplanade) which features a giant selection of cheesy New Orleans souvenirs, plus more cool cheap sunglasses than you've ever seen, two pairs for $5!

But if the weather's nice, after a full day of drinking and shopping, gravitate down to the **Mississippi River** and its romantic **Moon Walk**, named for former New Orleans mayor, **Moon Landrieu** (a good place to smoke pot, if you're vigilant for bike cops). We also suggest taking the **Algiers ferry** (free for pedestrians and bikes!) located at the foot of Canal Street, across the Mississippi to interesting and quaint Algiers Point on the Westbank (ferry leaves New Orleans every thirty minutes, on the :15 and :45, from 6am to midnight).

Despite whatever hype, you will and should spend a day or two wandering unselfconsciously around the French Quarter, drinking before sunset out of your go-cup until you're tipping every street performer. Just promise us you won't party there the whole time.

The Abbey, on Decatur in The Quarter.

CENTRAL BUSINESS DISTRICT

(CBD)

Boundaries: Tulane Ave (north), Mississippi River (south) Canal St. (east), Lee Circle (west)

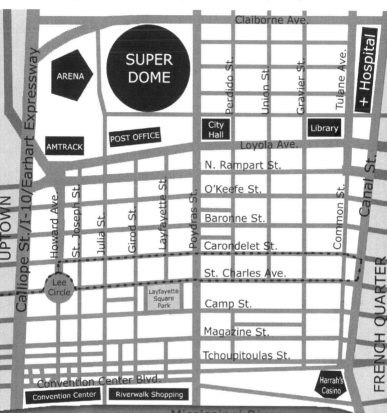

The CBD hosts all of New Orleans' tall office buildings, which would make any outsider think it's our "downtown," though it's actually the midway point between Uptown (*Garden District*) and lower 9th ward. (*Bywater*). The CBD boasts some good New Orleans restaurants, though many are open only during weekday lunch, catering to the working stiffs. Notable exceptions include **Emeril's** (*800 Tchoupitoulas St.*) and **John Besh's Luke** (*333 St. Charles Ave.*) and **Domenica** (*123 Baronne St.*), and new dining spots seem to be opening there every week. **The Julia Street arts district** is continually open and nice to stroll down, though there's more cutting-edge, street-level art elsewhere in the city. In the end, you'll probably get all you need of the CBD on your streetcar tour, rolling between the giant old New Orleans office buildings on your way to better vistas.

The portion of the CBD nearest the river is called the **Warehouse District**, though many of the area's old 19th century warehouses were converted into condominiums (what type of weirdoes, in one of the most architecturally beautiful cities in America, choose to live in condos?) The Warehouse District is also home to the **Contemporary Arts Center** (*900 Camp St.*) and the **Ogden Museum of Southern Art** (*925 Camp St.*), as well as the venerable **Howlin' Wolf** rock club and, (in the Wolf's old space) the **Republic**. The condos and the Convention Center have served impetus for added nighttime fun options in the Warehouse District, in the form of music clubs and upscale restaurants.

DAN FOX

UPTOWN

Boundaries: Carrollton Ave. (north); Mississippi River (south); Carrollton at the river bend (east); Lee Circle (west)

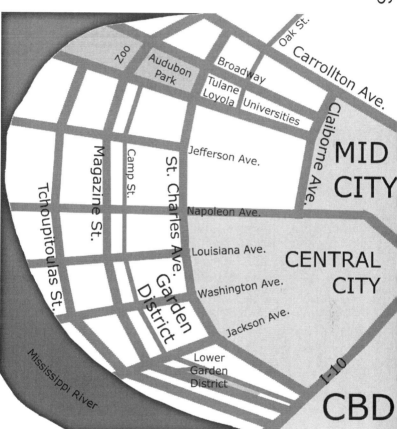

The designation "Uptown" is mostly an umbrella term to describe the neighborhoods and areas of New Orleans that are west of "above" Canal Street. Uptown is seen (perhaps wrongly) as one of the more stable parts of the city in terms of population and crime, and is attributed with a lot of the same qualities as most places called "uptown" are (that is, a lot of it is fancy). In the **Lower Garden District** (the unkempt, solitary cousin to the "Upper" Garden District) you will find the dog-and-bum friendly **Coliseum Square Park (**intersection of Coliseum and Euterpe streets), plus numerous cool dive restaurants and bars. In the late 90's, *Utne Reader* dubbed the LGD America's hippest neighborhood. You may judge for yourself.

Jackson Ave. is the downtown border of the Garden District proper: the walking-tour part of Uptown, where you'll find most of Magazine Street's shops, plus the **Vampire Lestat House** *(1239 First St.)* and **St. Louis Cemetery No. 1** (3421 Esplanade Ave).

On the other side of Magazine Street from the Garden District is the **Irish Channel** and its community center-bar-restaurant **Parasol's** *(2533 Constance St.)*. The Irish Channel, along with the Lower Garden District, has seen somewhat of a resurgence since the St. Thomas housing projects were shut down. It's also known as the "Sliver on the River," since Katrina, due to it being actually above sea-level and one of the least-ravaged parts of town (The world famous Wal-Mart, where NOPD and looters alike helped themselves to flat-screen televisions and ammunition, is on Tchoupitoulas St. and Jackson Ave.)

Between Louisiana and where the River turns is simply Uptown, and becomes more residential, save for hot spots like the corner of Napoleon and Magazine. The area between the River and Carrollton is the home of **Tulane** and **Loyola Universities**, and lots of college-kid-friendly restaurants and bars. A lovely New Orleans moment can be had on the veranda of the **Columns Hotel** (*3811 Saint Charles Ave.*), just downtown of Napoleon; put on your seersucker, sit under the huge white columns and watch the streetcar roll by while you pretend you're Queen of Carnival.

MID-CITY

Boundaries: The Canal Streetcar line (starts at the riverfront in the French Quarter at Esplanade), turns onto Canal Street and heads through the Central Business District, before continuing into the heart of Mid-City.

Mid-City sits midway between the Mississippi River and Lake Pontchartrain – making it a prime area for flooding, were it not for Esplanade Ridge, one of the longest, highest shelves in the city (which didn't really save it from the floods of '05). This mixed-income, visually stunning neighborhood was damaged badly by Katrina, but has managed to come back strong. The Fairgrounds horse racing track hosts every **Jazz Fest**. **The New Orleans Museum of Modern Art (NOMA)** is still representing in vast and wondrous **City Park**. Mid-City also hosts many mini-hoods you can and should explore. Gawk at the big houses, which are as gargantuan as Uptown, but colorful and unpretentious. During the day, Mid- City is mostly safe and beautiful; still, it's easy at night to wander somewhere you might not want to be.

FAUBOURG TREMÉ

(TREM-MAY)

Boundaries: Claiborne Ave. (north), Rampart St. (south), Esplanade Ave. (east), Canal St. (west)

The relatively small but culturally invaluable Treme neighborhood is famous for being the first area in America where Black people could buy and sell land, even as the country was still enmeshed in slavery. Its many corner bars, churches and funeral homes were the breeding ground for centuries of musicians to hone their horns and drums. In many ways, the Treme's unique energy – which has endured surprisingly well since the storm – is the biggest reason why New Orleans will always be "a Chocolate City," as former mayor Ray Nagin called it.

Along with a lot of great shotgun houses and corner stores (some of the best food in the city comes not from Galatoire's, but from various corner stores) Treme is home to several homegrown museums dedicated to celebrating African-Americans' cultural, historical and artistic achievements.

Treme is also where the biggest, most beautiful second-line jazz funerals occur. Regular churchgoers will be welcomed at traditional, very musical, New Orleans-style services at the country's oldest Black Catholic church, **St. Augustine.**(*1210 Governor Nicholls St.; 504-525-5934*).

ZS

LIVE MUSIC CLUBS

Music, food and drinking in the streets are the main attractions in New Orleans. The French Quarter definitely does not have the market cornered on music, with a huge percentage of its offerings consisting of cover bands and drunken karaoke joints – although it is home to the excellent **Preservation Hall** *and* **One Eyed Jacks**. *In any case, great clubs thrive in every neighborhood.*

12 Bar

CBD, 608 Fulton St., 504-212-6476; 12barnola.com

Set in the business district and named after the most popular chord progression ever written, 12Bar hosts mostly blues, jazz and funk, but will book pick-up acts from comedy shows, to a recent Halloween one-off wherein Jello Biafra sang rock covers of New Orleans R&B standards.

All Ways Lounge

Marigny, 2240 St. Claude Ave. 504-218-5778; marignytheatre.org

The longtime home of Cowpokes, a gay bar with a rootin'-tootin' theme, this space was taken over by a more punk-rock-friendly contingent (and by punk rock, we mean tall-bike-riding, accordion-playing, train-hopping punk rock). It's lately been blowing up with shows featuring the more established Bywater acts such as **Ratty Scurvics**, **Mary Go Round** and **Why Are We Building Such a Big Ship?**, plus DJ "sissy bounce" nights. The back room still is the home base of the community **Marigny Theatre**, which hosts all manner of local, alternative performance.

Bacchanal

Bywater, 600 Poland Ave., 504-948-9111; bacchanalwine.com

Hosts live jazz and serves up creative foods in a verdant outdoor courtyard.

Banks St. Bar

Mid-City, 4401 Banks St., 504-486-0258; banksstreetbar.com

Before this Mid Ciry neighborhood even had power, Banks St. Bar was serving beer by candlelight. (You can see photos of the flood damage on the bar's website). Lots of local bands play – from R&B to electro to reggae to metal – and there's rarely a cover. It's small enough that the bands run their own PA, but the club often hosts multiple shows per day – a rarity even in New Orleans. Be warned that, in New Orleans, rock shows can often be very poorly attended, so if you go to Banks St, bring a friend to talk to just in case. They've also got free red beans and rice on Mondays and free oysters on Thursdays. Not much else is around in that area (as of this writing) except a few pioneer neighbors living on sadly torn streets in beautiful sagging buildings, but Banks St. is a great spot to see where and how people in New Orleans actually live.

BJ's Lounge

....

Bywater, 4301 Burgundy St., 504-945-9256

Charles Bukowski would have loved BJs as, listening to the great jukebox with a host of colorful alcoholic musician types, one feels as if they're sitting in a black plastic ashtray. On Thanksgiving and other holidays, BJs hosts live music and potluck dinners with smoked duck and crawfish mac-n-cheese, among dozens of other neighborhood dishes. No credit cards.

ROBIN WALKER

The Round Pegs (feat. Ph Fred) rock out beneath the Circle Bar's famous giant clock ceiling.

Circle Bar

CBD, 1032 Saint Charles Ave. (on Lee Circle); 504-588-2616; circlebarnola.com

Under the watchful, um, eye of General Robert E. Lee's backside (his statue sits atop an obelisk in the middle of the roundabout) stands this teeny-tiny bar in a ramshackle old house that looks as if it's about to fall down. The interior's cozy – it fits maybe 75 people – and the booking runs to homey, necessarily intimate shows from local artists' side projects and young bands on the come up. There's almost always a show, almost never a cover, and the jukebox – courtesy of original owner **Kelly Keller**, a legendary underground-rock personality who passed away in 2004 – boasts one of the finest collections of punk, garage and Louisiana R&B and soul as ever there was. At press time, however, the club is still closed for renovations.

Chickie Wah Wah

Mid-City, 2828 Canal St., 504-304-4714; chickiewahwah.com

Named for the song recorded by **Huey "Piano" Smith and the Clowns** in 1958 for the French Quarter-based **Ace** label, this Mid-City joint books a cheerful grab bag of homegrown acts, from **Evan Christopher's** trad-jazz to **Jumpin' Johnny Sansone's** barroom blues, and host late-late night gigs during Jazz Fest. They have a small bar-food menu, including a sloppy Cuban sandwich, for soaking up booze. Plus, it may be the closest bar featuring live music

in proximity to Orleans Parish Prison.

Carrollton Station

Uptown, 8140 Willow St., 504-865-9190; carrolltonstation.com

Carrollton Station is kind of like Cheers for laid-back Uptown roots-rockers – like the '60s folk-rock queen **Susan Cowsill**, who does a monthly set here called "Covered In Vinyl," where she and her band perform a favorite album track by track. It's near the universities, but the crowd skews a little more grown-up, and they have a full menu of greasy, delicious bar food. The bar's owners started a small foundation after Katrina to distribute grants to local musicians in need.

Country Club

Bywater, 634 Louisa St., 504-945-0742; thecountryclubneworleans.com

As hot as New Orleans is, there are not nearly enough swimming pools. Unless you sneak into a hotel pool (which we all do often) the Country Club's funky, nice, clothing-optional pool and hot tub area is one of your only options. The club's majority crowd is gay, with more of a mix of neighborhood people and service industry folks at night. The restaurant – which also serves a poolside menu – features surprisingly fancy snacks like seared mahi mahi with chutney and cilantro spaetzle alongside standard country-club fare (club sandwiches, chef's salad). $10 will get you in for a visit, while $299 will get you a year's membership. Ask about discounts for service-industry slaves, which are significant. Country Club randomly hosts concerts and film screenings as well, which leave you wondering why every nightclub doesn't have a nude pool.

Dragon's Den
·····································

Marigny, 435 Esplanade Ave.,
504-949-1750;
myspace.com/dragonsdennola

Up the precarious, twisty red stairwell you'll find a red-lit room with pillows on the floor. Out on the decorative iron balcony, you can still smell the club's signature blend of incense and sweaty, dancing bodies. After the flood, the Den, once a Thai restaurant with music upstairs, was sold to a crew led by local **DJ Proppa Bear**. Proppa installed turntables both upstairs and downstairs, where a second stage was also added. More electronic music parties featuring hip-hop, jungle, reggaeton and the like, were added to the club's already admirable roster of brass bands and New Orleanian alternative music.

JT

From hip-hop to jungle to jazz, rock and brass bands, the Dragon's Den hosts all things good.

MUSIC

N.O. MOMENT:

MISS ANTOINETTE, AND ERNIE K-DOE'S MOTHER-IN-LAW LOUNGE

Treme, 1500 N. Claiborne; 504-947-1078; k-doe.com/lounge.shtml

"Emperor of the Universe" Ernie K-Doe passed away in 2001, though he'll still greet you – in the form of a life-sized wax statue dressed in one of his old stage suits – if you visit the club. K-Doe had a hit in the '60s with the track "Mother-in-Law" and though that was his career high point nationally, locally he became a beloved icon for his flamboyant presence in the bars and as a DJ on WWOZ and WTUL radio. (Tapes of his old shows, during which he often sings over the records he's playing and hollers catch-

phrases like "Burn, K-Doe, burn," and "I'm cocky, but I'm good," are collector's items). The bar took more than five feet of water in Katrina, but was remodeled fairly true to the original quirky style. It's since been purchased by trumpeter Kermit Ruffins who's yet to reopen it. The bar's outside walls are completely covered with artist **Daniel Fusilier's** explosively colorful mural depicting K-Doe, his widow Antoinette, and their favorite local music personalities. Before she too passed away on Mardi Gras morning 2009, Antoinette took over the lot next door and turned it into a floral paradise with outdoor seating (though traffic does roar right past on busy Claiborne Avenue). Over the 2007 Christmas season, Ernie K-Doe had a surprise posthumous hit when his 1970 song "Here Come The Girls" was used in a popular TV ad for the British drugstore chain, Boots.

JT

DISCLAIMER

Mother-in-Law Lounge was recently bought by trumpeter Kermit Ruffins, but has yet to reopen.

MUSIC

DAN

Hi-Ho Lounge

....

Marigny, 2239 St. Claude Ave.,
504-945-4446;
myspace.com/hiholounge

This veteran of New Orleans'
underground scene is where
many of the city's weirder acts
– including two of our biggest,
Quintron and the late **Morning
40 Federation** – came up.
In the years before Katrina,
though, it became almost
comically dirty. You could hear
the ice machine rattling through
the PA. The flood proceeded to
kick things around quite a bit,
but the Hi-Ho's new owners
used their insurance money
in the best way possible; the
club now boasts a sweet sound
system, raised wooden ceilings,
rotating exhibits by artists from
the Bywater and beyond. It's
now clean without feeling
sterile, and serves pizza along
with other bar foods. Best of all,
they still have a go-go cage in
which you can dance.

The Hi-Ho Lounge on
St. Claude (seen here
with bouncer Victor) is
the nicest low-budget
concert venue in New
Orleans.

Hookah Café

....

French Quarter, 309 Decatur St.,
504-943-1101; hookah-club.com

Like some vast velvet lounge
for middleclass vampires, with
intelligent lighting and a top-
shelf bar, Hookah's one of those
rare upscale-ish places that's
still soulful and comfy. Various
forms of organic electronic
dance music populates much
of the music calendar but you
could also catch live acts from
bounce rap to the occasional
rock show, all while smoking
quality hookahs.

Howlin' Wolf
·····································
*CBD/Warehouse District, 907
S Peters St., 504-529-5844;
howlin-wolf.com*

The Wolf is a hard place to pin
down. Once a major contender
in the city, its status has been
significantly shrunk over the
years by House of Blues who,
with ClearChannel money
behind them, can outbid any
truly local club. The Wolf has
its own faults, being just one
sprawling room, with nowhere
to go but outside for any kind of
break (thank God you can drink
outside here!). But the sound
is pristine, and the dude who
owns it – who also manages the
Rebirth Brass Band – has been
championing the local scene
forever. This may not be where
you wander over looking for a
random good time, but if they
book a show – they love brass,
and local hip-hop – it will sound
perfect.

Le Bon Temps Roule
·····································
*Uptown, 4801 Magazine St.,
504-897-3448;
myspace.com/4801magazine*

Le Bon Temps is a ramshackle
old honky-tonk with a couple
of pool tables, a great, greasy
kitchen and local music almost
every night with no cover.
Former owner **Pepper Keenan**
(of **Corrosion of Conformity**
and **Down** fame) used to let
local bands practice here during
the days just after Hurricane
Katrina to encourage the scene
to rebuild. The booking is now

generally just good-time rock
n'roll, free oysters on Friday
and a regular free weekly gig
(Thursdays, at press time) from
the **Soul Rebels Brass Band**
that's been shaking the walls
there since forever.

Mid-City Lanes
Rock n'Bowl
·····································
*Mid-City, 3000 S. Carrollton Ave.,
504-861-1700; rockandbowl.com*

Rock n'Bowl has been a city
institution for decades, and
is a favorite for New Orleans
natives who want to two-step
and jitterbug on the dance floor
to bands like the late, legendary
Snooks Eaglin and his big red
guitar, who played here almost
monthly until his death in 2009.
It's one of the quintessential
local New Orleans experiences,
and it's usually the spot that
zydeco and Cajun acts play
when in town. The rhythm
section always gets a boost from
the all bowling rolling during
the sets, and the annual Elvis
birthday celebration is quite
a show. It's likely you'll see
owner John Blancher – in the
turquoise '50s-style bowling
shirt that's the club uniform –
dance on the bar or take over
the mic from whatever band's
onstage. Rock n'Bowl recently
moved a few blocks from its
time-honored spot to a new
locale, but somehow managed
to bring the spirit with it.

New Orleans Healing Center

ZS

New Orleans Healing Center

....

Marigny, 2372 St. Claude Ave.; neworleanshealingcenter.org

With a stated mission of providing services and programs promoting physical, nutritional, emotional, intellectual, environmental and spiritual well-being, the 55,000 square-foot Healing Center also hosts entertainment, with drinks, at the Café Istanbul Performance Theater. The Crossroads Arts Bazaar and The Gallery Spaces both feature the work of local artists and artisans. Other options inside this center include the Island of Salvation Botanica, Fatoush Coffee & Juice Bar, The Movement Room Dance Studio, Wild Lotus Yoga, Worldwide Concepts Travel agency, a co-op grocery store and bank and more.

One Eyed Jacks

....

French Quarter, 615 Toulouse St., 504-569-8361; oneyedjacks.net

Downtown's premier independent rock club has a delicate balance of punk and swank, with ornate flocked red wallpaper that evokes equal parts Storyville and '70s porn. (They've also got an excellent collection of velvet nudie paintings). The building started life as a theater, which means the gently raked floor of the showroom guarantees generally awesome sightlines from anywhere in the 400-capacity space. The calendar usually includes equal parts big-name indie-rock and shows from big local players in the bohemian scene. Thursday night is a screamingly popular '80s DJ night, and Mondays usually feature low-key free early shows in the front bar.

Preservation Hall

....

French Quarter, 726 St. Peter St. between Bourbon & Royal, 504-522-2841; preservationhall.com, preshall.blogspot.com

For only $10-$15, listen to real Traditional Dixieland jazz with an impeccable pedigree with few distractions (no booze, no smoking). Music starts at 8pm and runs until midnight. The band plays several 30-minute sets and your ticket is valid all night. But there's far more to the Hall than just trad-jazz: under the stewardship of **Ben Jaffe**, son of Hall founders **Allan and Sandra** (way back in 1961,) Pres Hall has been steadfastly keeping it fresh and exciting. Look for viral Youtube videos of the band kibitzing on tour, collaborations with the crafty **New Orleans Bingo! Show** and a series of album releases featuring the band's talented heavyweights doing their own thing.

Saturn Bar

....

Bywater, 3067 St. Claude Ave., 504-949-7532; myspace.com/saturnbar

Saturn Bar (whose awesome old-school neon sign, but not the bar building, appeared in the movie *Ray* through the miracle of CGI) is a bona fide New Orleans legend. Its original owner, the famously irascible **O'Neil Broyard**, was legendary for his dislike of making change, talking to customers and basically running a bar in general; he filled the club to bursting with a collection of priceless New Orleans art, keepsakes and garbage, the distinction between which is up to the individual. Broyard passed away in 2006, and the bar is now run by his nephew **Eric Broyard** and Broyard's niece **Bailee**, who cleaned up the cat pee smell but otherwise left its fabulous junk-shop vibe intact. It's now one of the best spots in town to see local music, from avant-garde jazz to metal, and they still sell the iconic calendars, T-shirts and day planners that helped cool bohemian types worldwide wink at each other in that "Yeah, I know the Saturn Bar" way. It's also across the street from **Mr. Quintron's Spellcaster Lodge**, and as such, a fine place to get a drink when the Spellcaster's makeshift bar is down to half a bottle of cranberry juice and no ice at 3 a.m.

Siberia

....

Marigny, 2227 St Claude Ave., 265-8855

A small, empty black rock club with a pooltable and a tight PA. Heavy on the heavy: garage rock, punk, metal and all else wild from around the world. Kick-ass food in the back (see Restaurants).

Sidney's Saloon

....

Treme, 1200 St. Bernard Ave.,
504-947-2379

North Claiborne and St. Bernard Avenues, which run perpendicular to one another in Treme, were once the heart of New Orleans' black commercial district. St. Bernard in particular was a major neon strip, full of bars and music spots. In the '60s, the construction of the I-10 overpass, which runs over Claiborne like a gloomy, noisy canopy, cast a pall over the 'hood. St. Bernard still is home to a host of neighborhood bars that cater mostly to an older African-American crowd; Sidney's, recently purchased by horn player **Kermit Ruffins**, stands at the center of the strip. There's often live music, occasionally Kermit himself– and when he's not playing, he might be cooking up a pot of red beans with turkey necks. Also, **Preservation Hall** banjo player **Carl LeBlanc** can often be heard across the street at the **Perfect Fit**.

DAN F

Musician, producer and Piety Street Recording Studio owner Mark Bingham sits in on the banjo with accompanist, Freddie "King Gong" Brink.

N.O. MOMENT :

SPEAKEASIES

More underground clubs/bars/house-party spots exist in New Orleans than this book's authors know about. But here are a couple we're allowed to reveal.

The Pearl

....

Bywater

This house/speakeasy, The Pearl, by the river on Desire, is a huge, haunted-seeming Mardi Gras den-cum-junk shop full of Carnival paraphernalia and every other odd or end you could imagine. At concert parties lasting well into the next day, The Pearl hosts all types of crazy neighborhood bands and DJs – plus gourmet tacos and oysters. Pearl parties are rarely advertised, but if you're hanging out in Bywater, feel free to inquire around.

Cousin It's wife has either a pre- or post-party drink at The Pearl speakeasy in Bywater.

St. Roch Tavern

Marigny, 1200 St. Roch Ave; 504-945-0194

A 100% authentic no-hype dive bar where you will feel charmingly unsafe while meeting some fucked-up locals and hearing music from under-the-radar local bands, ranging in styles from harmonica blues to metal. There are always dogs, cheap bar food, and sometimes blood on the floor.

The Republic

Warehouse District/CBD, 828 South Peters Street; 504-528-8282; republicnola.com http://nola.com

Once a place solely for college kids spending a lot of their parents' money, in recent years the Republic has matured a little. It's still a little fratty, but shows by everyone from Niko Case to Of Montreal, plus extraordinarily packed local indie rock shows (especially for the Throwback series, which features a local band opening up for a wild DJ dance party) make The Republic a good enough local alternative to House of Blues.

Schatzy (who doesn't always look this "out of it").

Vaughan's Lounge

Bywater, 4229 Dauphine St.,
947-5562

This dilapidated-looking saloon deep in the Bywater is without a doubt one of the city's best bars. Serious touring musicians from **Will Oldham** to **The Rolling Stones** have come down on Thursday night to see and hear proud viper and Louis Armstrong facsimile **Kermit Ruffins and his Barbecue Swingers** (or some fill-in brass band or other) get Vaughan's dancing, which Ruffins has done for nearly two decades. In recent years the college kids found out about Kermit and they jacked up the door fee, as well as downgraded the free half-time barbecue to beans and rice. But on regular nights Vaughan's is generous with the free grub given any halfway good excuse, and at Kermit's halftime, in the bar's shadows, there are still plenty of other smokey treats to be shared.

Zeitgeist Multi-Disciplinary Arts Center

Uptown, 1618 Oretha Castle Haley Blvd., 504-827-5858,
504-352-1150; zeitgeistinc.net

This place is more like a community center than a real theatre. Still, it maintains its role as the premier place to consume alternative film, dance, theatre and avant-garde music. Often, it's the only venue to catch the more outré film festival favorites on a big screen with the added benefit of knowing you're supporting truly marginal, bohemian culture. They host everything from the annual touring Sex Workers Art Show to a human rights film festival.

BIN WALKER

Rotary Downs plays Tipitinas

N.O. MOMENT:

FRENCHMEN ST.
THE CURRENT MUSIC CAPITAL OF NEW ORLEANS

Similar to Austin's famous 6th Street (but less overwhelmingly touristy, we think) Frenchmen Street is back-to-back clubs and funky, inexpensive restaurants. There's no real reason for us to itemize every Frenchmen eatery and bar featuring free music; Frenchmen is to be enjoyed as a whole. Just go down there and wander around. But if'n you are interested, here are six favorite spots:

Revelers dance outside the 3 Muses restaurant bar and concert venue

ZS

13 Restaurant and Bar

Marigny, 517 Frenchmen St., 504-942-1345

Vegetarian dining is one area where New Orleans comes up kinda short. But whether or not you partake of animals (not even seafood? Really? C'mon!), 13 Restaurant and Bar (owned by the owners of **Molly's** bar, where you'll surely end up, whether we suggest it or not) is located in the midst of Frenchmen Street's many clubs, and open as late as possible. They serve great drinks alongside carnivorous deli sandwiches, vegetarian options such as gourmet pizzas and salads, and original concoctions like tater-tot nachos ("tator-tachos") covered in cheese and black beans. Especially during the summer, 13's frozen Irish coffee (topped with a sprinkle of grounds and shaved chocolate) is unbeatable.

MUSIC

Adolfo's

....

Marigny, 611 Frenchmen St., 504-948-3800

Adolfo's Louisiana Italian restaurant doesn't host music, but it's such a great place that we can't bear to leave it out (Plus, you can hear the bands from the bar downstairs coming through the floor). For those whose budgets sometimes allow travel to cool places, but then dictate frugality once they get there, Adolfo's will make you feel kingly. The amazing seafood you might get in the Quarter's well-advertised fine dining places costs only half as much at Adolfo's, and with some small extras included. As of this writing, a giant grouper filet stuffed with crawfish, crab *and* shrimp *with* a salad and perfect hot garlic bread, was $16.95. Upstairs from the colorful, dark and snug **Apple Barrel** *(609 Frenchmen St., 504-949-9399)* blues dive, with a view out over the music clubs of Frenchmen Street, Adolfo's is absolutely European.

Adolfo's

JT

Blue Nile

....

532 Frenchmen St., 504-948-2583; bluenilelive.com

This extremely eclectic club with two nice stages and sound systems (separate door costs) hosts everything from live hip-hop MCs and DJs (**DJ Real and Earl the Pearl** Saturdays at 11pm, and the **Soundclash** beat battle the second Saturday of each month), dancehall nights hosted by **DJ T Roy**, lots of traditional New Orleans music (from **Kermit Ruffins** to various **Nevilles**), a marginal amount of indie rock, a few fashion shows and even a quirky improvisational jazz series. That being said, their programming varies so wildly, it's advisable to make sure you know who's playing before you pay the cover.

dba

....

Marigny, 618 Frenchmen St., 504-942-3731, drinkgoodstuff.com

ZS

Drummer Simon Lott and friends get the crowd at club DBA on Frenchmen St., to lay on the ground.

During the week there's often no cover for dba's well-curated roster of New Orleans music, jazz vocals to rowdy funk to straight-ahead rattling blues. This is also where **Stevie Wonder** chose to pop in after Jazz Fest, and countless others. Right next door to Snug Harbor.

Dragon's Den

....

Marigny, 435 Esplanade Ave., 504-949-1750;
myspace.com/dragonsdennola

Up a steep, precarious twisty red stairwell you'll find a dim, red-lit room with pillows on the floor – anchored on one end by the bar and the other by a wrought-iron balcony overlooking the grassy Esplanade Avenue neutral ground and the mouth of the lower Decatur dive-bar strip. After the flood, the Den (once a Thai restaurant with music only upstairs) was sold to a crew led by local **DJ Proppa Bear**. Proppa installed turntables both upstairs and downstairs, where a second stage was also added. More electronic music parties featuring hip-hop, jungle, reggaeton and the like, were added to the club's already near-perfect roster of brass bands and alternative music.

Snug Harbor

Marigny, 626 Frenchmen St., 504-949-0696; snugjazz.com **ZS**

Though more adventurous spirits may find some of the jazz shows here too staid, Snug is nonetheless promoted as the city's premier spot for big-name local and international jazz acts, with sets nightly at 8 and 10 pm. Jazz patriarch and educator **Ellis Marsalis** plays here with his quartet monthly. The other half of the building is given over to a casual-upscale supper club focusing on steaks, burgers and Gulf seafood. Tip: the often-pricey upstairs show is usually broadcast on closed circuit TV you can watch at the downstairs bar.

Yuki Izakaya

Marigny, 525 Frenchmen St., 504-943-1122

Hesitant to write much about this comfy upscale-ish Japanese place on Frenchmen, since it hasn't been here long. But for the sake of their menu of late-night fried dumplings, yakitori and sake (modeled after the after-work spots Tokyo businessmen booze it up in) plus unusual live music (Yuki is the best place to catch cellist **Helen Gillet's** French chanson combo, **Wazozo**) and good DJs, we hope Yuki sticks around.

N.O. MOMENT:

FAUXBEAUXS, GUTTERPUNKS AND OTHER STREET KIDS

New Orleans was once famous for attracting what we called **"gutterpunks,"** a breed of street kid buskers who, aesthetically, combined the oft-prophesized *Blade Runner/*

ROBIN WALKER

Mad Max look, with the slovenliness of truckers and sitcom TV dads: canned beers dribbling down stained white t-shirts onto soiled jeans. The gutterpunk breed overpopulated lower Decatur Street after Katrina, begging from locals who'd just lost their homes – when most of those kids, when they aren't wasted, are healthy enough to outrun you in a foot race. Luckily this was temporary, as lately, many mildly-rebellious American kids who *would have* grown up to become gutter punks, have evolved into what Bywater locals now refer to as "**fauxbeaux**," a French Louisiana word meaning "fake hobo."

The Bywater and Marigny fauxbeauxs are snowbirds who arrive in town around Mardi Gras each year, stay through festival season, then fly (or hop a train, they'd have you believe) back up north. The fauxbeauxs' entire aesthetic is sepia-toned: defiled black and dirty white lace dresses for the girls, while guys prefer small hats, suspenders and clam digger pants, also grubby. An old-timey look, with the addition of tattoos. Some of them purport to live a soulful Kerouacian existence, while most have access to credit cards to buy nicer things, but just dig the look. Locals also refer to fauxbeauxs as "chimney sweeps," "depression-era paperboys," "funkballs," and a hosts of other names. Aside from a core of silly, sloppy, crazy drinkers who sneak their own beer into bars (thus gypping the music scene out of money), the fauxbeauxs generally don't get as wasted as the gutterpunks, and so are mellower. Also, unlike gutterpunks, fauxbeauxs do not beg. Instead they play music, often for donations. Often the music is imitative of an old timey porch-stomp sound. But some of their female vocalists perfectly mimic beautiful old phonograph-era singers, and a few of the more ambitious fauxbeauxs have honed their chops in New Orleans and worked toward well-paying gigs for the Jazz Fest crowd.

But fauxbeauxs' cultural contributions are too often obscured by a well-observed xenophobia; like pigeons flying over houses looking for the gloppy white streaks that will tell them where it's safe to land, fauxbeauxs come to town, dig in with the folks who dress like them, and rarely communicate with the many other interesting creatures around them. Visually, they certainly blend into shabbily elegant New Orleans, but fauxbeauxs could stand to act more local, by embracing the concept of southern hospitality.

NEW ORLEANS BANDS 2011

The official music of new millennium New Orleans is not jazz, funk, blues, or any genre that can be described in just one word. Well, there's rap, but. Many New Orleans musicians create a true sense of the city without sounding like old, traditional New Orleans music. Mardi Gras is just as big an influence on many of these bands, but more the sheer visual spectacle of Carnival than the traditional sound (though any rock band desiring to sound "heavy" should study New Orleans high school marching units). The city's seasonal banjo-strumming accordion-tooting fauxbeaux bands even manage to sometimes subvert genres (other times they just mimic Tom Waits). Even the city's abstract/experimental/noise music scene is genuinely entertaining and fun in a way that can definitely be attributed to living where we do. The true heart of New Orleans music is not jazz, funk or blues, but rather, originality! Here is an overview of New Orleans music in the 2000's:

A Hanging

myspace.com/ahanging

Grindcore-esque metal band with a hot chick singer. Their own myspace description, all caps: "WILDCAT STUCK IN GARBAGE DISPOSAL."

A Living Soundtrack

myspace.com/alivingsoundtrack

Electronics-driven instrumental indie rock act that mixes cinematic, experimental sound with a video projector for live performances.

Theresa Andersson

theresaandersson.com

Andersson came to prominence as a talented fiddle player and singer who, with the help of other songwriters, hybridized various forms of American "roots music" into something almost her own. Recently, with the release of *Hummingbird Go!* Andersson began following her own unique muse, a muse who wanted her to use loop pedals and other modern instruments to create something truly unique, and very beautiful. It doesn't hurt that she's one of the best violinists in a state full of fiddle players, and that her voice is as strong as any American Idol contestant. Her current one-woman-band is standing-ovation worthy.

Au Ras Au Ras

myspace.com/tessbrunet

Tess Brunett, former drummer for **Deadboy and the Elephantmen** and **the Generationals**, creates a sensual, singing-focused panorama of electronics and guitars.

The Bally Who?

myspace.com/theballywho

The two Cajun brothers **Duffourc, Jacques and Renee**, have their hands in a lot of different pies, as video artists, Jackson Square painters, and as the two core members of The Bally Who? To call them a cross between **Pink Floyd** and **Flaming Lips** would be to have only seen one show (or heard their one album, *Keep On Dawn*). Each Bally Who? musical experience is different than the next. If one show features just the brothers, rocking guitars along to electronics, the next will be a full marching band in matching uniforms. Their native status also mean the brothers have many fun, creative friends who create a fun atmosphere at their shows.

Ballzack

ballzack.com

This Armenian Westbank-born comedian-turned-rapper has cycled through genres including nerd rap, New Orleans bounce music, and a sort of **Violent Femmes** post-hip-hop. Incredibly popular, Ballzack fills the main room at House of Blues. For all his shtick, Ballzack always brings the theatrics, and the hits, and the crowd is always moved.

Big Blue Marble

myspace.com/bigbluemarble

Big Blue Marble revolves around singer-songwriter **Dave Fera**, who descended into New Orleans from Boston, and has since become a unique, low, deadpan voice on the scene. Fera is backed by a carefully orchestrated rock band in the vein of **My Morning Jacket**, or a mellow **Neil Young**. Big Blue Marble's secret weapon is lap steel guitarist **Michael Blum**, whose volume pedal creates swooping accents in the band's otherwise earthy rock.

BlackBeltBand

sickroomrecords.com/Releases/SRR053.htm

Having played in various combinations for the last 12 years, the members of Blackbelt have produced a signature style utilizing acoustic, electric and electronic instrumentation to create a mix of experimental rock, blues, post-punk, reggae, and movie soundtrack.

Big History

www.facebook.com/bighistorymusic

Dual female singers lead this fresh-faced, wildly popular electro-pop-rock group. Backed by a mountain of laptops and synths, Amanda Wuerstlin soars on violin and Bret Bohnet rocks the electric/acoustic drumkit.

Big Rock Candy Mountain

bigrockcandymountain.net

Rock with fuzzy guitars, analog keyboards, ultra-sweet harmonies, distorted bass-lines, and techno drum beats. Fun and loud.

Bipolaroid

facebook.com/bipolaroidmusic

Bipolaroid's garage rock drips down the walls. Over the course of many years and many lineups, **Ben Glover's** musical vision has evolved into something truly psychadelic, bent and beautiful. The band's most recent incarnation features garage-rock icon **King Louie** on drums.

Blind Texas Marlin

myspace.com/blindtexasmarlin

A feral cat style songwriter/screamer/guitarist who has come a long way towards perfecting the 'badass while almost falling apart' aesthetic.

Ray Bong

bongoloids.com

Actually from Lafitte, Louisiana, Ray is as close to a Hunter Thompson-esque character as anyone you'll ever meet (even in New Orleans): a drug freak psychedelic noise musician who, because he's also a wealthy independent engineer who put four kids through college, has attained guru status. Ray can be seen at rare solo shows pounding away like a caveman on totally unrecognizable analog gear (the Tri-Wave Generator, the Coron, the Superstar 3000 toy guitar). Or else, more often Bong provides soundscapes for electro-rock-n-R&B singer and guitarist, **The White Bitch** *(myspace.com/thecreamywhitebitch)*.

The Buttons

myspace.com/thebuttonsnola

New Orleans' version of **Kraftwerk** – live electronic dance rock played on keyboards and Theremin – Buttons was once a steadier band but now comes and goes on the scene, with the two members maintaining more of a presence as DJs at fun, youthful dance parties.

Caddywhompus

caddywhompusband.com

Two-piece (drums/guitar) math-pop with handsome vocals.

Chef Menteur

chefmenteur.org

A live space-rock band named after a famous New Orleans highway, Chef Menteur's drone-oriented "songs" are built around murky loops and samples, and a tight rhythm section.

Clockwork Elvis

myspace.com/clockworkelvis

This Elvis cover band has an extensive personal narrative vision that connects the story of *A Clockwork Orange* to **Elvis Presley**. It's not immediately apparent in the performance–straight-ahead Elvis songs played honestly and with love (but not jumpsuits)– but you can ask lead singer **Elvis DeLarge**, if you want the whole hypothesis. Actually, we suggest it. The band often play shows with local burlesque troupe the **Billion Dollar Baby Dolls**, led by DeLarge's wife, **Reverend Spooky LeStrange**.

The Consortium Of Genius
....

consortiumofgenius.com

Part band, part multimedia weirdness, the C.O.G. is a gaggle of costumed mad scientists who carry on the tradition of New Orleans' famous TV host **Morgus the Magnificent** in musical form while, according to them, trying to take over the world. With songs like "Lab Coat" and "Science Fight," they definitely have a shtick, and the rocks shows are highly theatrical. Sometimes C.O.G shows feature original films, which include their fifth member, a cartoon robot.

Quintron and the Drum Buddy

N.O. MOMENT:

ANXIOUS SOUND PRODUCTIONS AND NOISE GUITARIST ROB CAMBRE

Since 1997, guitarist Rob Cambre's **Anxious Sound Productions** has been the first name in adventurous modern music booking, with shows usually pairing international cult musicians with some hot New Orleans cats – including Cambre, who fits himself into almost every show he books. Luckily his **Sonic Youth** meets

JT

Japanese-noise freeform guitar work is often worth it. Cambre's sets run the gamut from solo improvised electric guitar to more structured acoustic pieces to off-the-cuff groups with drummers, bassists, saxophonists, dancers and poets. His intermittent **Dry Bones Trio** with **Endre Landsnes** (drums) and **Bill Hunsinger** (bass) plays ferocious, high-energy music touching on aspects of free jazz and rock, while **The Death Posture** features *Borbetomagus* guitarist **Donald Miller** and *butoh* dancer **Vanessa Skantze**. More recently he's taken up with "garage gospel" group R.**Scully's Rough 7** and **Bones**.

You never can tell where Anxious Sound sex-rockers might pop up, but if you're in town for more than a day or two, the chances are good you can catch one. However, there are a few Anxious Sound events you can mark on your calendars. On January 30th of each year, Cambre hosts the *Anxious Sound Holiday HO-Down* at the Hi-Ho Lounge: a blow-out of adventurous improvisers from New Orleans, Baton Rouge, and Mississippi, usually including the likes of **James Singleton** (bass), **Helen Gillet** (cello), **Bruce Golden** (perc/electronics), **Donald Miller** (guitar), and of course Cambre himself. More recently, Cambre also concocted the *Sound-Circus* concert series (a more high-level production supported in part by an **Arts Council** grant) at The Big Top arts center, featuring an international roster of improvisers that has included **Han Bennink**, **Ken Vandermark**, **Ab Baars**, and many, many others. In 2009, Cambre also helped bring about the first New Orleans installment of the **No Idea Festival**, curated by Austin-based percussionist **Chris Cogburn**, and featuring musicians from Baltimore (**Bonnie Jones,**) Mexico City (**Mario de Vega,**) and Zurich (**Jason Kahn**). In short, if you enjoy difficult and/or complicated listening, look for the Anxious Sound label on the product.

Note – if you enjoy strange, experimental sounds, also check out purveyors of freaky jazz and software experiments like drummer **Justin Peake**, keyboardist **Brian Coogan**, trombonist **Jeff Albert** or sax man **Dan Oestreicher**, just to name a few scatterjazz players in the New Orleans strange music conspiracy. Albert curates frequent improvisational jams (at the time of publication) under the umbrella of the **Open Ears Music Series**.

Country Fried

countryfried.net

The best New Orleans has to offer in the way of twang, Country Fried is technically impressive, with virtuosic strings and perfect vocal harmonies in the old-fashioned acoustic country string band tradition. Some of the city's soul and R&B influences have also snuck in, and Country Fried's live covers of Southern rock and contemporary alt-country acts like **The Band, Lucinda Williams, Gram Parsons** and **Little Feat** add some fire to the mix.

Dave Gregg

facebook.com/people/Dave-Gregg

Primarily a street performer, Gregg plays New Orleans standards and other jazz and funk with one hand strumming a guitar around front, the other hand picks another guitar behind his back, while his bare feet play the bass. Turn your back and you'd never know.

Dash Rip Rock

dashriprock.net

The 25-year-old world's greatest bar band – hits include "Locked Inside a Liquor Store With You" and "(Let's Go) Smoke Some Pot" – is also edgy enough to release albums through **Jello Biafra**'s label, **Alternative Tentacles**.

Debauche

debauchemusic.com

Russian-born Yegor Romanstov, backed by his "Russian Mafia Band," croons and bellows rocking drunken versions of Russian folk songs, some more than a century old, written by prisoners and gangsters, hooligans, orphans and gypsies. One crowd favorite tells of lesbians who marry in jail then escape, only to be killed.

Phil DeGruy

guitarp.com

DeGruy only comes out into the light if he doesn't see the shadow of his "guitarp" on April Fool's Day. The "guitarp" being the guitar DeGruy invented, wherein a tiny audible 11-string harp built into the body is played simultaneously or in syncopation with the other six strings. His constant dry but subversive sense of humor and otherworldly playing was described by former Zappa and David Lee Roth axeman Steve Vai as, "John Coltrane meets Mel Brooks at a party for Salvador Dali." DeGruy also shares the stage with fellow hilarious guitar wizards, **Jimmy Robinson** and **Cranston Clemments** in the band **Twangorama**.

Die Rotzz

myspace.com/dierotzz

A loud punk rock power trio who make fun musical mess. Die Rotzz also does double time as **Guitar Lightnin' Lee's Thunder Band**, which means they, improbably, hang out with Fats Domino sometimes, and play blues like a broken steamroller.

Mike Dillon

myspace.com/mikedillonpercussion

This tricky percussionist and vibes man has played in jam-band-friendly musical experiments including **Les Claypool's Frog**

Brigade, and his own **Mike Dillon's Go-Go Jungle**. In New Orleans, he's often seen in combinations with **Galactic's Stanton Moore**, jazz/funk drummer **Johnny Vidacovich**, and bass weirdo **James Singleton**. A big favorite of the **Bonnaroo** crowd.

Doomsday Device

myspace.com/doomsdaydevice

Weird, aggressive rap-esque music made on a Playstation and other funky computer toys. Their description: "an abstract thought that stems from 2001: A Space Odyssey, and ends somewhere within the sonic grace of the Ramones."

Dummy Dumpster

myspace.com/dummydumpster

A punkish, noisy, unpredictable anything-goes project started in Chalmette, La. in 2001. The microphone is mounted in the singer's decorated homemade shoulderpads, allowing him to rip around the room and petrifying the crowd as he sings.

Steve Eck

myspace.com/steveeck

A dark singer-songwriter and guitarist, Eck bends compositions that could be played straight into beautiful and wholly unique shapes, then backs them with amazing New Orleans players from all over the musical spectrum. You won't

party and dance to this music, but it kicks the ass of most New Orleans party music.

Empress Hotel

parkthevan.com/empresshotel

Brothers **Ryan** and **Eric Rogers** (guitar/drums), **Julie Williams** (keys) and ex-Silent Cinema singer **Micah McKee** play 70s-esque folk music with touches of funk and punk. Stream of consciousness lyrics power dynamic vocal melodies.

EyeHateGod

myspace.com/eyehategod

Since 1988, New Orleans most famous (or at least most important and tenacious) punk-metal band has been called the innovator of doomcore, sludge, and stoner rock (*see N.O. Moment.*)

Fat Stupid Ugly People

Grindcore, punk, thrash. Big, loud, wild. Fat, stupid, ugly.

Felix

myspace.com/felixnola

Wild, messy, blues-punk band with a secret weapon organ player who coats the guitar-and-drums in beautiful, creepy textures. (*see Blind Texas Marlin*)

MUSIC

MUSIC

N.O. MOMENT:

TIP THE PERFORMERS!

New Orleans is a haven for people who can do things well – but usually just one thing, to the point where they're otherwise unemployable, despite their musical talent. Music is many New Orleanians' sole source of income. So, this may seem over-obvious – and good for you if it does! – but some people don't realize: TIP EVERY PERFORMER that you enjoy! Not the weepy old terrible folk singer whose too-loud amplifiers pollute the air around Jackson Square, but that silver-painted ghost mime lady you took a picture of, you DAMN WELL better tip her. Or if you enter a club with no cover charge, even if you stop in to just for a second check out a band you approve of, *definitely* tip them. You wouldn't pull that in a strip club, don't pull it on Frenchmen Street.

ZS

N.O. MOMENT :

HELEN GILLET

You've never witnessed a cellist rock this hard. Dynamic and experimental but unpretentious and fun, Gillet plays jazz, Medieval music, she sings French chansons and "musettes" in her band **Wazozo**, uses loop stations in her wild solo act, and helps reconstruct the abstract orchestra pieces of bass wiz **James Singleton** – to name just a few of her many successes. If you came here for music, Helen is a must see.

ROBIN WALKER

Gal Holiday and her Honky Tonk Review

galholiday.com

Undeniably retro, and undeniably pretty, Gal Holiday presents high-quality recreations of old country music.

Generationals

generationals.com

A strikingly pleasant version of a well-worn indy style: guitars shimmer behind passionate dual vocals swamped in reverb. Like a third generation **R.E.M.**, or a more hearty **Galaxy 500**.

Glasgow

glasgowband.net

Stalwarts of the New Orleans scene, brothers **Sam** and **Jack Craft** use eclectic instrumentation like electric violin and cello, creating rock akin to **ELO**, **Queen**, and **Bowie**, all filtered through a **Zappa**-esque absurdism.

Glorybee

myspace.com/glorybeeglorybee

The most popular band in New Orleans before Katrina-- a self-described "children's nightmare hip-hop cheerleading squad" – Glorybee was washed away by the flood at a time when locals could have used their ambitious, hyper fun, Mardi Gras-influenced dance rock. Eventually the two core members, **Bradley and Nancy Davis**, returned home and reformed the band with Bradley's amazingly talented relatives. The new Glorybee isn't as ass-shaking, and lacks the electronic beats. But the band's new material proves they didn't need all the costumes and confetti to make something truly beautiful and unique.

Gov't Majik

myspace.com/govtmajik

By fusing free-from jazz and mind-melting atmospheric elements, this 10-piece afro-beat band aims for the psychedelic majesty of **Fela Kuti**, while whipping up a world groove dance frenzy.

Gravity A

gravitya.com

Self-described as "funktronica," this jam band quartet combines New Orleans funk, drum n' bass breaks, and trippy trance.

Green Demons

greendemonsrock.com

Sci-fi surf punk featuring **Todd Voltz** and **Gwendolyn Knapp**, singer/guitarists with a shared sense of humor. Voltz is also an actor seen in comedies including **Harold and Kumar**, and **Waiting** (a good Comedy Central flick about restaurant work).

Husband and wife Bradley and Nancy Davis of brainy, soulful, downright weird band, Glorybee.

Guitar Lightnin' Lee

guitarlightninlee.com

Born and raised in the Lower Ninth Ward (and lifelong friends with **Fats Domino**'s son **Antoine Jr.,**) Lightnin' studied blues guitar with masters like **Jimmy Reed** and **"Boogie" Bill Webb**, and has palled around with every major artist to come through New Orleans. His scrappy band of white punk rockers also make up the very loud band **Die Rotzz**. Together, they make sloppy, fuzzy, unhinged blues that will make you spill your drink and slap your mama.

Haarp

myspace.com/haarpnola

Sludge/doom metal, championed by **Pantera**/**Down** singer **Phil Anselmo**. Reviewer Brandon Bowers puts it best: "Haarp blends a molasses chugging onslaught of traditional sludge metal, with bard-like tale telling, mature harmonic composition, and low, guttural vocals" (see essay on metal).

N.O. MOMENT:

NEW ORLEANS' WORLD-FAMOUS HEAVY METAL SCENE

The South has been married to heavy metal music since before the Civil War. Okay, maybe that's a slight exaggeration, but New Orleans' metal musicians are some of the city's biggest ambassadors – and some of the least heralded within the city's borders. In the early '90s, Louisiana natives **Pepper Keenan** and **Phil Anselmo** were both living outside the city and playing in hugely successful groups (**Corrosion of Conformity** and **Pantera**) which would influence generations of rockers to come.

Metal band Thou rock long hair and flying-V guitars.

"You know, I can remember being nominated four different times, back when I was in Pantera, for Grammys," Anselmo told the *Gambit* in a 2009 interview. "And they'd have on the news all the local New Orleans stars who were nominated. My name was never up there. And nothing against them – I even went to Lakeview high school with **Harry Connick**, and summer camp. But Pantera, we sold more records."

In 1995, Keenan and Anselmo started the band **Down**, whose first album *NOLA* went gold. Its drop-tuned, grinding drone, influenced by acts like the **Melvins** and honed in grungy New Orleans VFW's by groups like **Eyehategod,** would become the distinctive, influential and oft-imitated Southern metal sound. "When the Down thing started, we focused on making the licks real slippery and not mechanical," Keenan said. "I don't know if it was 'Southern,' but the whole attitude was very influenced by New Orleans, the feel of it, the greasiness. Back in the day, the Meters were a very vicious band," Keenan continued. "You couldn't touch them. They had some songs that were heavy as lead. But I personally did not want to play a hollow-body guitar and jangle around.

Nor did **Eyehategod** singer/squealer **Mike IX Williams**. Williams "wanted to do a punk band that played really slow, and kind of pissed everybody off, with lots of feedback and noise," Williams said. "It ended up being taken seriously, and we ended up getting a record deal." Williams' other band **Outlaw Order** existed on a virtually parallel timeline to Eyehategod, and features almost the same members. Williams lost his house to a fire after Hurricane Katrina and left town, but he's now back in New Orleans, playing in his bands and working at Anselmo's **Housecore** label (*thehousecorerecords.com*), which just released a self-titled demo from Anselmo's longtime black-metal-influenced project **Christ Inversion**, and a vinyl EP from **Arson Anthem**, a thrash/hardcore band featuring Anselmo, Williams and **Hank Williams III**. At the time of publication, the label also plans releases from **Arson Anthem**, the Metallica-influenced, Memphis-based **Evil Army**, and the up-and-coming New Orleans sludge-metal band **Haarp**, whom Anselmo says are, "The best fuckin' New Orleans band I've seen since the late '80s."

Though many of the city's die-hard metal clubs have vanished (RIP Dixie Taverne), New Orleans still boasts a healthy local metal scene, which includes **Hawg Jaw**, **Spickle**, **Thou**, **Mars**, **Face First**, **A Hanging**, **Tire Fire**, and dozens of others. Booking companies **86'd Productions** (*www.myspace.com/86dproductions*) and **Noxious Noize** (*www.myspace.com/noxiousnoizeproductions*) both book metal and hardcore almost exclusively, multiple shows every week. The websites *www.noladiy.org* and *www.nolaunderground.com* are also excellent sites to find out where to go if you're feeling the need to "throw the goat" while in town.

Happy Talk Band

myspace.com/thehappytalkband

Happy Talk is mostly frontman **Luke Allen**, whose bittersweet songwriting captures the bohemian, downtown New Orleans life where bartenders, strippers, junkies, artists, musicians and other similar sorts live, drink and die. Allen, a guitarist, plays in several combinations, from a raw, electric alt-country/punk combo to a gentle ensemble with cello and pedal steel. His economy of words will break your heart.

Hawg Jaw

myspace.com/hawgjaw

Hardcore music for people who don't think hardcore is interesting enough, Hawg Jaw was formed in 1996. The vocals are more expressive than most metal, and the heavy music is twisted and brutal (see essay on metal).

The Help

reverbnation.com/ thehelpfromneworleans

Barbara Menendez fronted New Orleans new wave/punk band **The Cold** in the early 1980s. Three decades later, her band the Help cite (English) Beat, Blondie, X and the Buzzcocks among its influences.

Hurray for the Riff Raff

hurrayfortheriffraff.com

The best example of Bywater train hopper music. Cat Power-esque singer/banjo player **Alynda Lee** actually did learn music by participating in train-hopping culture. As a result, HFTRR use acoustic instruments to spin 6/8 waltzes and modern country ballads about life's perils.

The Hons

www.reverbnation.com/thehons

Classic, classy, love-and-sex-centric power pop, best exemplified on the band's perfectly chizled gem of an album, To Skyward.

Hot Club of New Orleans

hotclubofneworleans.com

The Hot Club perform the swing era music of **Duke Ellington,** plus **Django Reinhardt,** and **Stephan Grappelli** among others, yet avoid sounding like a museum piece by infusing the music with their own modern sensibilities. In keeping with the classic format of this music, Hot Club lacks a drummer – but will still make you dance.

Jealous Monk

myspace.com/jealousmonk

Funk-infused hip-hop band led by one of New Orleans' greatest freestylers, **Intelligence**, and DJ/MC **Jermaine Quiz**.

King Louie

myspace.com/ kinglouieandhisrocknroll

Harahan's most famous rock n'roller – perhaps more well-known for his unpredictable behavior than his music – has played in a laundry list of revered local garage bands. It's fun to watch Louie as a one-man-band play double bass and guitar simultaneously. Plus, as a native, he has an tight circle of friends who dance their asses off at even the most minor of his shows.

Little Freddie King

littlefreddieking.com

Little Freddie King is the genuine article – a real-deal bluesman with a hardscrabble bio, a guttural, menacing mumble and a ferocious gutbucket guitar. King, who was shot twice on two different occasions by the same wife (and stayed married to her,) released a record on **Fat Possum** a few years ago, and more recently, put out the excellent *Messin' Around The House* record of **R.L. Burnside**-style remixes.

The Local Skank

myspace.com/thelocalskank

Talented all girl ska band (with a dude drummer). Check out their delicious 2010 pin-up calendar.

Lovey Dovies

theloveydovies.net

A less ostentateous take on the Dinosaur Jr. aesthetic of big melodic fuzz. When not in town playing at The Saint or Circle Bar, they have the balls to regularly drive down and tour Central and South America.

Mars

myspace.com/marsdoom

Since 2006 Mars has made slow simple stoner doom metal for the end times.

Tom McDermott

strdigital.com/mcDermott.html

McDermott, a crafty and gifted pianist whose main idioms are traditional jazz and Brazilian *choro*, is most often seen around town with clarinetist **Evan Christopher,** messing with people's expectations of classic genres. His original work has a strong sense of humor and experimentation that smarty-pants jazz fans – including uptight moldy-fig traditionalists – will nonetheless totally enjoy.

Kelcy Mae

kelcymae.com

Poetic roots music about the American South with acoustic instrumentation that'll surely appeal to the Canadian North.

Alex McMurray

alexmcmurray.com

New Orleans could use more singer/guitarist/songwriters like McMurray, a gigging musician who knows how to please New Orleans audiences, but on his own original terms. His are also usually humorous, bawdy stories filled with deep pathos.

McMurray performs as a soloist, with the trio **Tin Men** (with a tuba player and **Washboard Chaz**), as the leader of the large nautical-themed **Valparaiso Men's Chorus**, and as a featured guitarist in **Happy Talk Band**, among many other incarnations. He is also a producer of **Chaz Fest** (see Festivals).

Meadow Flow

myspace.com/meadowflow

Psychedelic, dreamy, rain-soaked lullabies, light summer jams molding pretty noise into pop.

Metronome the City

metronomethecity.com

This instrumental band of New Orleans natives has played together since high school. With guitar, bass, drum kit, keys and effects they somehow sound like a DJ seamlessly mixing together dub reggae, metal, and **Thrill Jockey**-style indie rock.

Microshards

myspace.com/themicroshards

Usually a ferocious, bass-wielding/tape-manipulating one-man-band, Microshards has recently enlisted a drummer and keyboardist to enhance his over-distorted rock instrumentals. On other recent occasions the band has instead gotten trashed, disrobed, and just thrown their instruments around the room in a way that's somehow honestly artful and engaging.

Mikronaut

This solo artist and DJ drinks a lot of cough syrup, and makes extremely listenable, drugged-out minimalist dub-influenced electronica on various Casios and a four-track cassette recorder. When performing, Mikro runs said four-track into effects pedals and creates live remixes like the old dub masters. Mikronaut, however, is a snowbird, and can mostly only be seen during New Orleans' winters.

Morella and the Wheels of If

myspace.com morellaandthewheelsofif

This haunting and romantic co-ed cabaret dispense free **Lucid Absinthe** from the stage, and sometimes also offer a peek at Vincent van Gogh's lost ear. Projections show original films, video, and photography created by musical siblings **Aeryk Laws** (pianist/ composer/ singer/guitarist) and **Laura Laws** (writer/singer), and their singing and writing partner **Anastacia Ternasky**. As much an "act" as a "band," Morella has performed at the **DramaRama** theatre fest and the annual **Fringe** multi-media fest. (see *Theatre*) The band can also be caught at **Circle Bar,** Saturdays at 6 p.m. (perfect time to start drinking absinthe).

MOTO

myspace.com/moto

Hooky garage rock with song titles like "2-4-6-8 Rock 'n'

Roll," "Gonna Get Drunk Tonight," and "Flipping You Off With Every Finger of My Hand." The phrase, "so dumb they're brilliant," can be found in several MOTO reviews. Unfortunately for New Orleans, MOTO's usually on tour.

Mr. Go
....
mrgoband.com

A mostly laid back party grunge band with a 60s fetish and a pension for studio experimentation.

MuteMath
....
mutemath.com

Though MuteMath somehow became literal arena rockers without ever participating in the local music scene (how does that happen?) these closet-Christian emo rockers are currently New Orleans most famous rock band.

Mynameisjohnmichael
....
mynameisjohnmichael.com

Not very New Orleansy, MNIJM is the type of big, multi-member indy rock group that's so in vogue now all across the country. MNIJM distinguished themselves by writing and recording a song-a-week through 2007, then having fans pick which songs would grace their debut album, *The People That Come and Go*.

Narcissy
....
narcissy.com

This rarely seen (and thus relished) garage rock outfit posesses a startling sense of humor and a spastic yet smart stage presense. "The perfect thing for people who like this sort of thing," reads the website.

Necro Hippies
....
myspace.com/necrohippies

From *Maximum Rock-n-Roll*: "Screaming and slurring over mostly mid-paced thick and dreary riffs, and stompy drums. This is also one of those bands that are able to come up with the simplest of riffs that still make you clench your fists." A favorite at Siberia.

NooMoon Tribe
....
noomoon.net

Noomoon is famous for their *Land of Nod* stage of local bands and other masochists at each year's Voodoo Music Experience. In '09 the group or performers and artisans moved their stage into the French Quarter for a wild mid-October multi-media music and arts festival to benefit the **New Orleans Musicians Clinic**. The Tribe's other events include *Exotica New Orleans*, a fetish model and lifestyle convention in April *(exoticaneworleans.com),* and *Bunarchy New Orleans*, a bunny-costumed bar hop around the French Quarter and Marigny, held on the Thursday before Easter to benefit the LASPCA.

MUSIC

N.O. MOMENT:

THE NEW ORLEANS BINGO! SHOW
WWW.NEWORLEANSBINGOSHOW.COM

J. LLOYD MILLER

Part cabaret, part game show, part heartbreaking balladry, Bingo! is an ensemble cast of leering costumed characters led by eccentric **Clint Maedgen**. The band started out playing shows for free in the back room of a fried-chicken joint on Decatur St. in the French Quarter (where Maedgen worked delivering food on his bike) and have since moved on to curate their own huge tent at the annual **Voodoo Music Experience**. The crew has racked up a million other not-so-small local and national accomplishments in between.

Bingo's sets feature a combination platter including but not limited to Theremin playing, seedy clowns and mimes, original short films, a couple rounds of actual bingo with the crowd, plus quirky songs about life in the New Orleans' booze-gutter. Bingo upped the ante a few years ago and gained mad crossover appeal after pairing up with the venerable **Preservation Hall Jazz Band**. Maedgen, a conservatory-trained saxophonist, sang for Pres Hall for several years before the band lost their clarinetist, and Clint began filling in, even though he'd previously never played clarinet. Nowadays, the two bands – old-school and modern sides of the same New Orleans coin – participate in many peculiar collaborations that any visitor would be blessed to witness. Check website for show dates.

The Other Planets

....

theotherplanets.com

When people talk about New Orleans jazz, they're usually referring to the trad/Dixieland stuff you hear at venues like **Preservation Hall** or the Palm Court Café–but in fact, the city has been an off-and-on hub of avant-garde space-jazz weirdness for decades, helped along by proponents like **Alvin Batiste** and **Earl Turbinton**. The Other Planets continue this non-traditional tradition with bizarre cosmic explorations, sarcastic, spacey freak-rock soundscapes and **Sun Ra**–inspired trips through the sonic spaceways. And sometimes, there's a light show.

One Man Machine

....

myspace.com/onemanmachine

Alone or with a group (likely assembled that week), **Bernard Pearce** swears by a seat-of-the-pants improvisational style

Out-there Zappa influenced mega-musicians The Other Planets collect donations for Red Cross after hurricane Katrina.

not seen much in rock circles. Usually based on one consistent loop and a few memorized poetic lyrics, One Man Machine's music, and the players who realize it, all vary wildly from show to show.

The Pallbearers

....

myspace.com/neworleanspallbearers

It's always Halloween for New Orleans' original sicko horror punks The Pallbearers, who've been trafficking in loud guitars and blood since 1997. More than a couple shows have ended with the singer going to the hospital.

67

N.O. MOMENT:

RATTY SCURVICS

Ratty Scurvics' Black Market Butchers with Rob Cambre and R. Scully. (*myspace.com/rattyscurvics*)

Ratty comes in many forms. In his one-man-band **Singularity**, Scurvic's hands pound stacks of keyboards while his feet pump the snare and bass drums. After ending Singularity in 2007 (the only one-man-band to ever break up), Ratty started this Bywater multi-media presentation featuring members of **Fleur De Tease** and **Morning 40 Federation**, plus singer **Meschiya Lake**, guitarist **Rob Cambre** and others. The band's first album, In Time was produced by **John Porter**, an auxilary member of Roxy Music who produced most of The Smiths' singles. In whatever capacity Ratty plays, the spectacle is always amazing, but Ratty's powerful, thoughtful music always gets the party dancing and transcends the spectacle. Ratty is emblematic of how modern New Orleans music often defies categorization.

N.O. MOMENT:

RIK SLAVE

Rik Slave:
rockcitymorgue.com
rikslaveandthephantoms.com

ZS

On and off since 1986, Rik Slave has been the revered frontman for numerous projects – with his brother Greg Terry in the bent country group **Rik Slave and the Phantoms**, and more recently **Rock City Morgue**. RCM is mostly simple and to the point ala the Ramones or Mistfits, with jaunts into Nick Cave territory when former White Zombie bassist Sean Yseult takes to the piano.

Panorama Jazz Band

panoramajazzband.com

Composed of stellar local players, Panorama dress in traditional brass band captain's hats and ties, but that's as far as the band's traditionalism goes. Its signature sound is classic New Orleans street parade music mixed with a healthy, exotic dose of Balkan brass and other rare forms.

Proud Father

myspace.com/proudfathermuse

Thoughtful ambient noise and rythmic patterns performed live on various electronics.

Pumpkin

myspace.com/pumpkin

Youthful synth-driven, washed out post-punk with loud guitars and video collage.

Quintron and Miss Pussycat

quintronandmisspussycat.com

Outside of New Orleans–especially in the weirder parts of Europe – Mr. Q, is beloved as a maker of strange analog electronic dance music. Swirling roller-rink organ, bleeps and bloops from his unique invention the Drum Buddy and simple drum machine patterns, complement backup vocals from his companion, Miss Pussycat, who often performs original psychedelic puppet shows before the duo's concerts. One of Q's electric pianos once belonged to deceased singer **Ernie K-Doe**, which is fitting since Q's music owes a great deal to the New Orleans R&B piano tradition (not to mention **Prince**).

R. Scully's Rough 7

myspace.com/rscullysrough7

Gravel-voiced former party-boy frontman of the **Morning 40 Federation** (New Orleans' favorite drinking band, who still reform from time to time, especially at **VooDoo Fest**) wipes the smirk off and moves closer to the heart for songs he considers "garage gospel." **Rob Cambre** (lead guitar), **Ratty Scurvics** (piano) and singer **Meschiya Lake** (whose awesome backup wailing brings the group closes to their gospel goal) round out this supergroup of punk-influenced musicians as talented as any of the city's traditional bands.

MUSIC

R. Scully's Rough 7

Rhodes

myspace.com/ rhodesmakesshittymusic

Pre-recorded tracks, live drum machines and percussion toys back this one-man-band caterwauling southern electro pop, ala Britney Spears. At Siberia or Saturn Bar, Rhodes will invade your personal space. Don't attend his shows in your expensive clothes.

Rotary Downs

rotarydowns.com

Rotary Downs are one of New Orleans' few straight-up indie rock bands. Their popularity has lately grown as they've shed their Pavement influence in favor of a slightly psychedelic but even-tempered sound, featuring eclectic instrumentation.

Sick Like Sinatra

myspace.com/sicklikesinatra

Electro-disco sex rock with a great frontman.

James Singleton

The most amazing standup bassist you've ever heard or seen. Mop-haired, eternally youthful 50-something Singleton has played with everyone from **Ellis Marsalis** to **Clarence "Gatemouth" Brown** to **James Booker.** But unlike so many other of New Orleans' best modern-day musicians, Singleton is also original, daring, and multifaceted, leading otherworldly outfits like **Astral Project** (with drummer/kook **Johnny Vidacovich), 3Now4,** and the **James Singleton String Quartet**, featuring wild cellist **Helen Gillet.**

Skate Night

reverbnation.com/skatenight

Queer electro-pop-punk group.

Smiley with a Knife

Quirky yet sleek instrumental rock that tempers more jocular, tickling tunes with other eerily emotive numbers. Smiley With A Knife initiated the first annual **New Orleans Instrumental Fest** in March 2009.

Slow Danger Brass Band

slowdanger.com

A large group of punkish downtowners, many of whom study music at UNO, Slow Danger play in the brass band style but rather than flow free, they perform compositions, including original songs, with minimal improvisation. Unlike other brass bands, Slow Danger also switch moods: some is danceable, and some is downbeat. For the brain and the booty.

Stix Duh Clown

Stix Duh Clown

....

Original bluesy folk songs. With his makeup literally tattooed onto his face, Stix strums and sings in either a Tom Waits growl, or sweeter folk croon, while playing bass drum on an old suitcase. Stix also fronts the bands **My Graveyard Jaw**, and **Death By Arrow**.

The Special Men

Special Men became popular years ago, playing a huge catalog of New Orleans R&B classics in an almost grungy guitar-based style, with Bingo's **Clint Maedgen** on sax. They returned recently without Clint, but with free red beans, every Monday at BJs (4301 Burgundy St., 504-945-9256).

Spickle

myspace.com/spickle

Ferocious four-piece instrumental band possessing sick chops. Heavy as metal, but without any of metal's corny trappings. Spickle is one of several bands powered by guitarist **Paul Webb** who owns **Webb's Bywater Music**.

Sun Hotel

sunhotelsounds.com

Hazy melodious, post-gospel music featuring ambient guitar and four-part vocal harmonies singing lyrics of love and loss.

Supagroup

reverbnation.com/supagroup

This established party metal group surely doesn't want to be "underground": high energy, ultra tight, big rock, never cheesy unless **Chris Lee** (husband of bassist **Sean Yseult**) and company know you'll laugh along. Check out their web TV show *Amped!*

Suplecs

Fun, heavy rock, now 10-years strong. Suplecs' debut album "Wrestlin' With My Lady Friend," was released by **Frank Kozik**'s label, **Mansruin Records** in April of 2000, and the video for the song "Rock Bottom" played on MTV's Headbangers' Ball. Suplecs always do an insane, free show at **Checkpoint Charlie's** each Fat Tuesday.

Terranova

terranovarocks.com

Catherine Terranova movd to New Orleans from Baltimore in 2008 to start a garage rock band with native **Michelle Lacayo** of **Manwitch**. The two can also be seen on a Muses parade float, playing with **Sue Ford** in the all girl Mardi Gras party band Pink Slip.

Thou

noladiy.org/thou

Down-tempo stoner metal. Fucking awesome (see essay on metal).

The Unnaturals

myspace.com/theunnaturals

Super tight rockabilly surf group.

The Way

....

myspace.com/thewaynola

Groovy classic guitar rock with no guitars, in a new-wave vein.

The White Bitch

....

myspace.com/thecreamywhitebitch

Admittedly, the author's stage-name/band since 2001. Because of The White Bitch's roots as a one-man indy-R&B-rock act using just drum machine beats, shreddy guitar, and high-pitched vocals, Prince comparisons continue to dog him – even now, when his new big full band (with intermittent horn section) is far heavier and more psychedelic.

White Colla Crimes

....

whitecollacrimes.com

Fun, party-rockin' white boy funk rock group with an ironic anti-corporate theme.

N.O. MOMENT:

WHY ARE WE BUILDING SUCH A BIG SHIP?

myspace.com/whyarewebuildingsuchabigship

Multi-instrumentalist and former **Hurray for the Riff Raff** member **Walt McClements'** huge band, **Why Are We Building Such a Big Ship?** is definitive Bywater music: a theatrical, somehow ghostly amalgamation of swaying, rollicking accordions, horns, violins, voices, and drums. Like a lot of other downtown New Orleans music, Big Ship is strictly acoustic. But Walt's band – or, all of his bands, actually – avoid the "fauxbeaux" tag, by keeping at least a few toes if not a whole foot, in the modern. "I want to be in a new wave band, actually," says McClements. "But I just keep picking the wrong instruments. In high school I played in all these garage rock bands and I just got sick of carrying amps around and dealing with broken electronics. I thought: *I'm going to buy a banjo*." At the eye of the Big Ship storm, Walt sometimes sings into a microphone, but as his group loves to play outside – where crowds can gather and grow to any proportion – sometimes he just sings/shouts/screams his heart out over five horns and drums, and still somehow sounds very good. Walt also lends his accordion services to the well-established ethnic-music marching mashup that is **Panorama Jazz Band** (see *Bands)*.

Although many of his band members are N.O. transplants, McClement's groups not only seamlessly blend into New Orleans' raggedy, slightly grubby but still stylish charm, they've come to really define Bywater's modern-gypsy style and sound. Tourists in need of souvenirs documenting the new sound of New Orleans early in the new century should purchase Big Ship's first album (beautiful hand-screened 12" vinyl) *No Blood No Blooms*, released on **DJ Prince Pauper's Domino Sound Records** (a label based out of the record store of the same name, see *Shopping)*.

Regarding the band's name – which ain't biblical – McClements muses, "Some folks are pretty positive it's a comment on the building of the USS New Orleans a year after the storm – when the military's way of honoring New Orleans was to build a five billion dollar warship, when obviously we could have used some of that five billion dollars to rebuild the city… But that's not what the name is. The phrase was just in my mind as my fortune: to me it meant you don't have to have so much on your plate! Focus on just a couple of things!"

NEW ORLEANS RAP ARTISTS 2011

N.O. MOMENT:

BOUNCE
THE OFFICIAL MUSIC OF NEW MILLENNIUM NEW ORLEANS

As hip-hop evolved throughout the 1980s, New Orleans rap largely sounded like what was happening in the rest of the country: sing-songy, **Sugarhill Gang**-style rhymes over fat, methodical beats with soul and funk samples. That all changed drastically around 1991 when "Where Dey At," allegedly the first "bounce" song, was recorded in two versions: by **MC T Tucker** with **DJ Irv**, and then shortly after by **DJ Jimi** as "Where They At," produced by 70's R&B industry player **Isaac Bolden**. The lyrics to this, and the trillion bounce tracks that followed, called out, and demanded responses regarding, your ward, your school and your project. More often than not, the lyrics were also really,

Katey Red

ROBIN WALKER

really dirty, describing all things sexual in gleeful anatomical detail. With bounce, as with almost all other New Orleans party dance music, fun was stressed over art.

Bounce ruled New Orleans' clubs and block parties for years, though the only national bounce hit was **Juvenile's** "Back That Azz Up." Some of the zillions of pioneering bounce artists include **Partners-N-Crime**, **Ms Tee**, **Mia X** and **5th Ward Weebie**, whose track "F*** Katrina" captured the local sentiment after the storm. The Tupac Shakur of New Orleans, the late **Soulja Slim**, even recorded bounce tracks as **Magnolia Slim** before veering into more gangsta territory. But even today, New Orleans DJs regularly remix R&B radio hits with the manic, skittering "Triggerman" rhythm (a sample from the 1986 track "Drag Rap" by New York City's **Showboys,** that turns up in most bounce, and bears a remarkable resemblance to the tambourine clatter of Mardi Gras Indian rhythms) and the later the night gets, the harder and faster the beat trips and pounds beneath warbling ballads and lazy hip-hop cuts from **Usher** and **Lil Wayne**.

Bounce pioneer **DJ Jubilee**, still holds down at-least-weekly gigs playing bounce (check his Myspace) and has earned the title "King of Bounce." In 2003, federal courts ruled against Jubilee in a suit he filed against Juvenile, denying the claim that the Juve's hit "Back That Azz Up" was a blatant rip-off of his own "Back That Ass Up," a song he'd been performing for years. Juvenile made millions; Jubilee is still a teacher by day in the New Orleans public schools.

In 1999, Jubilee's **Take Fo'** record label (home to artists including **Choppa**) issued *Melpomene Block Party*, the first full-length release from **Katey Red**, a gay, transvestite MC from the Melpomene projects, a.k.a. the Melf. Jubilee sensed that Katey – 6-foot-2 and slender – had something exciting and new, and her decade of popularity has proved him right. Other gay bounce artists have followed on Katey's (high) heels, most notably **Big Freedia** and **Sissy Nobby**, both "sissy bounce" rappers who hold down the mic at **Club Caesar's**, and perform elsewhere at least four nights each week. Most recently the sissies have been booking huge shows at rock clubs like **One Eyed Jacks** in the French Quarter. To learn about bounce shows listen to hip-hop stations like **Q93.3** and **102.9 FM**, or stop by **Nuthin But Fire Records** (*1840 N. Claiborne Ave.*) to pick up flyers – they're not often listed in mainstream publications.

MORE NEW ORLEANS RAP ARTISTS

The following was written mostly by Daniel Perez aka Impulss, a mainstay mason in the construction and rebuilding of New Orleans hip-hop. He has recorded with or shared stages with almost all of the culture's notables from **Akon** *to* **Scarface** *to* **Digable Planets**

Daniel Perez aka Impulss

While jazz artists fight to keep their artform alive, New Orleans' rap scene thrives and grows (despite its being all but banned from some "community" radio stations and record stores that supposedly specialize in New Orleans music). Years before bounce exploded, complex rhyming and true-school MCing in New Orleans was the norm, with lyricists such as **Tim Smooth**, **Gregory D.**, **Bustdown**, **M.C. Thick** and **Legend Mann**. As Bounce gained more club attention, it also gathered the steady support of radio program directors and DJs who saw hip-hop and bounce as opposing values. Writers of finely woven multi-syllabic articulations were given marginal room to perform.

But now a new generation, raised with infinite digital music at their fingertips and thus room to grow beyond radio hits, has taken a front seat position once again in New Orleans: MCs who would find themselves more comfortable atop a **J Dilla** masterpiece than say, a **DJ Money Fresh** bounce mash-up. Today, hip-hop fans of all stripes can find the culture he/she loves represented upstairs at **Le Maison** and **Dragon's Den** (both on Frenchmen Street), **Hi Ho Lounge** (St Claude) and many other of the city's venues. The **Supreme Street collective** headed by **Cracktracks' Law** plays host to a sizeable amount of shows. **Truth Universal**'s Grassroots monthly event (Dragon's Den) marches on. The **Soundclash** beat battle hip-hop variety show still goes strong at the **Howling Wolf Den**. **DJ Tony Skratchere** and Poor Boy Productions sometimes promote the world-renowned DMC DJ battle for world supremacy in NOLA. The self-congratulatory nature of hip-hop found it's way to the creation of the 1st **Underground Hip Hop Awards** at the **Howlin Wolf** venue.

All this to say: New Orleans hip-hop scene is diverse and abundant. Sunday evenings, 93.3FM's "504 Radio" (which usually plays basic ClearChannel pop rap) features insightful New Orleans MCs. A list of some of those refreshing artists follows:

10th Ward Buck

myspace.com/10wardbuck

A young, upstanding entrepenuerial bounce rapper and concert promoter who got the game rolling with some of the first ever bounce concerts at the Airline Skate Center. New Mouth from the Dirty South Press recently released a coffeetable biography called Tenth Ward Buck: the Definitely Of Bounce. These days, along with sporadic shows, Buck owns and operates the restaurant Finger Lick'n Wings (Lower Garden District, 739 Jackson Avenue).

A.Levy

thehutstudios.com

Owner of **The Hut** studios who made a name with his catchy tunes and fire stage shows.

ATM

myspace.com/atmneworleans

Battle tested, local lyricist and freestyler known for his fast flow and emotional stage presence. The originator of New Orleans' edition of **Grind Time**, a national rap battle competition.

Caligula

reverbnation.com/caligulakrycek

Throw Orwell's book *1984* into a pot along with every conspiracy theory you've ever heard, every anti-depression med Big Pharma ever produced, your pervy neighbor's porn collection, a barrel of booze, a penchant for fist-fights and a collection of head banging beats...and you've discovered Caligula.

Curren$y

currensyspitta.com

Known for buddah-blown lyrics and laidback delivery, Spitta jumped the **Cash Money** ship to soar with his **Fly Society** crew and **Damon Dash**.

Dappa

myspace.com/yaboydappa

Palmyra Street Productions MC with star appeal.

Dee-1

dee1music.com

A young but very creative and real MC, who nonetheless

doesn't curse on his albums, and released a single called "I Hate Money." An impressive positive lyricist, Dee-1 is making serious waves.

DJ MC Microphone

djmcmicrophone.com

MC, multi-instrumentalist, resident DJ for **ATM**, local hip-hop producer, and bassist in local rock band, **Snuff Sugar**.

Eupham

A hip-hop movement composed of **Crummy, DJ Mike Swift**, **Lyrikill** and **Mercure**, giving the masses creative, quality hip-hop music that expands the genre.

Guerilla Publishing Company

guerillapublishing.webs.com

Consisting of **Elespee**, **Caliobzvr**, **D.O.N.**, **DJ Skratchmo**, **Private Pile**, **Suave**, **Juskwam**, **Prospek** (providing the sonic boom-bap landscape), plus many more who wave the flag, GPC is a hip-hop supercrew that stands apart from their contemporaries.

Jealous Monk (live band)

myspace.com/jealousmonk

Funk infused hip-hop band led by one of New Orleans' greatest freestylers, **Intelligence** and DJ/MC **Jermaine Quiz**.

Jimi Clever

jimiclever.com

Maybe New Orleans' most honest lyricist. Emotion and feeling pour alongside his high-pitched cadence, compound rhymes and perfect beat riding.

The Knux

theknux.com

New Orleans born and raised hip-hop/garage/breakbeat brothers who moved to sunny California after Katrina.

Lyrikill

myspace.com/mclyrikill

Wordy linguist of **Eupham** crew and one of the founders of New Orleans' monthly beat battle, Soundclash.

M@ Peoples' Collective

Indie rock/Hip-hop fusion band brought to you by local MC, **M@ Peoples** and members of New Orleans jam band **Gravity A**.

Mercure

myspace.com/jonmercure

Member of **Eupham** crew, co-host of the monthly Soundclash beat battle, and local producer, mixing synths, old-school R&B, and witty freestyles.

The Microphone Corivalry House Band

myspace.com/microphonecorivalry

Three-piece hip-hop band –

composed of **Soul Nick, Cash Moore** and **Chris a.k.a. Mr. Chelata** – that plays during the crowd-judged, tournament style, Microphone Corivalry MC Competition.

K. Gates

gateswave.com

They call him International Gates for a solid reason. The author of the "Black and Gold Saints Theme Song," has traveled the world over from Mecca to Amsterdam building his multi-continental hustle and shining superior lyricism.

Know One

knowoneshome.com

An experimental MC pushing the boundaries of creativity and musicianship. A **Media Darling** crew member, he was one of the first to arrive Post-Katrina and begin to rebuild not only the hip-hop scene but also the city itself, laying brick and mortar, floating sheetrock as expertly as he floats on a beat.

Koan

koanmusic.com

Lower 9th Ward MC of **E.O.E.** Known for the musicianship and topical depth.

Lil' Dee

myspace.com/lildeegodsgift504

Having gathered a well-formed fanbase through thousands of mixtape downloads, well-received music videos and a giant

billboard hovering over the I-10 as you drive into downtown, Lil' Dee has burned his brand into the New Orleans hip-hop scene.

Lyriqs Da Lyriciss

A smooth, young expert living up to his name and out-rhyming his elders.

Na'Tee

3dnatee.com

Winner of the Best Lyricist award at the **NOLA Underground Hip-Hop Awards**. (Editor's note: she is also smokin' hot!)

Nesby Phips

nesbyphips.com

Hailing from **Curren$y's Fly Society**, Phips is in NYC working with Ski Beats who's discography boasts a long list of hits in Hip Hop music.

TheSeKondElement

teamt2e.com

A multi-talented woman also known as KAMMs TheACE, she is smart on the mic, nice with the graphic design and visually precise with photography.

The Show

Mannie Fresh protege' from New Orleans East

Sess 4-5

myspace.com/nuthinbutfirerecords

Ninth Ward rapper Sess 4-5's tracks sound sorta bounce-ish,

The connoisseur of fine rhyme, Slangton Hughes.

TASLIM VAN HUTUM

with the lawn-sprinkler high-hats, but his Black Panther lyrics are dense; the same combo locals loved in late, great New Orleans rapper **Soulja Slim**. Sess is also the proprietor of **Nuthin' But Fire** record store *(see Shopping)*, which regularly releases mixtape CDs featuring all of New Orleans' best underground rap artists.

Soul Capital

myspace.com/soulcapital

Composed of **Ben Brubaker** and **DJ Miles Felix**, Soul Capital brings a fresh sound and style to the game with conscious, yet entertaining lyricism and beats that move the crowd.

MC Shellshock

myspace.com/mcshellshock

Shelley considers herself more a poet, which is probably true, but when she takes the mic, it's definitely hip-hop. Her costumes mean a lot to her, and her stage show usually features dancers that at some point lift her high in the air as she spits super memorable verses about New Orleans' dating pool, and its other precarious nooks and crannies.

Slangston Hughes

myspace.com/slangstonhughes84

The Connoisseur of Fine Rhyme, member of **Tygah**

Woods crew and head of **P.T.E. Productions** (local hip-hop promotions/event company). Lyrical MC taking his reverence for old school hip-hop and infusing it with contemporary elements

MC Trachiotomy

mctrachiotomy.org

On the scene for more than a decade, Trach makes intentionally garbled psychedelic hip-hop funk, heavily influenced by the odd genius of bands like the **Butthole Surfers** and **Captain Beefheart**.

Truth Universal

truthuniversal.com

Truth has been hustling and grinding not only within New Orleans but throughout the continental United States for ten-plus years. His monthly **Grassroots!** open-mic event takes place on the first Saturday of every month at **Dragon's Den**

Tygah Woods Crew

myspace.com/tygahwoods

New Orleans' version of the Wu-Tang Clan – at least structurally: five MCs (Slangston Hughes, Mr. J'ai, J-Dubble, Blaze the Verbal Chemist, D. Francis) unite with DJ Mike Swift to bring hip-hop music back to its roots.

Rap

MC Trachiotomy and his partner/guitarist El Tonios pose at a Mardi Gras den.

JT

Rap

N.O. MOMENT:

INTERVIEW WITH RAPPER JUVENILE
"AIN'T NOWHERE TO GO IN NEW ORLEANS."

Rapper Juvenile, born **Terius Gray** in the old Magnolia Projects in New Orleans' Third Ward, started recording bounce rap when he was barely out of junior high. Juvie made his first mark on national music with the **Hot Boys**, alongside **Lil Wayne**, and with several solo albums on **Cash Money Records** in the late '90s and early '00s. His 2006 release on Atlantic, *Reality Check*, debuted

Famous New Orleans rapper Juvenile (of "Back that Ass Up" fame), chillin in his Uptown recording studio, because there's nothing else to do.

AUBREY EDWARDS

at #1 on the Billboard charts. After a two-year post-Katrina hiatus in Atlanta, Juvie is back in his renovated house in Lakeview and making music in a brand-new Uptown studio, where we hit him up for an interview. Here's Juvenile's suggestions regarding your visit to New Orleans

What's your favorite memory of music in New Orleans, growing up?

I ain't gonna lie. The second lines, man. I lived like right on the corner of Freret and Louisiana, and there used to be days that were quiet-quiet. And all of a sudden, you'd be asleep and then you'd hear that music – bomp-pa, bom-pa – I'd hear people right in front of my door. I'd just come right outside on my porch. That was amazing to me. You miss it when you go out of town. Like when I was in Atlanta I was like damn, I ain't heard some second line in two years. It was funny about it – you could be anywhere in New Orleans and a second line would pop up, and you'd be stuck there for a minute or however long it'd take to get around it. It's crazy.

If you were telling a visitor to New Orleans a couple of places to go that's not your average tourist spot, where would you tell them to check out?

I don't go nowhere, damn. Go to Riverview on a Sunday, that's the only thing I can think of. Cause really there ain't nowhere to go round here anymore.

Really? Like if you had a friend coming into town?

I wouldn't have a friend comin' in from outta town; I'd meet them somewhere cause really ain't nowhere to go right now in New Orleans anymore. Where else is there besides the tourist spots?

Do you ever go out to a club when you're not playing here?

Shit, these spots here, you gotta have a gun. So if I do go out it's gonna be to somewhere the tourists go.

What about some tourist spots then?

Man. I'd go to the **Tropical Isle** (*721 Bourbon Street*) and get a Hand Grenade. And that's the truth. Get me a cigar from the cigar spot on Bourbon. I go to the **Acme Oyster House** (*724 Iberville Street*) at least once a week. Or another spot up on St. Charles is the **Superior Grill** (*3636 Saint Charles Avenue*). I love that spot. That's my spot.

What local music would you recommend a visitor pick up when they're in town?

Definitely **Partners N Crime**. Definitely **Nutt da Kidd**. There's a lot of local artists down here that I like. Get some old **Soulja Slim** music, and when they get the music, go to **Peaches Records** and get it, in the old Tower Records place. Shirani (Rea, owner) got all my old records.

DJs, DANCE CLUBS, AND RADIO STATIONS

Some fans of traditional New Orleans music have no time for DJs, believing that, 'DJs aren't real musicians' blah blah blah. Regardless, many popular and downright important DJs improve the city. Like our better musicians, most of our DJs strive for originality as a more circuitous route to popularity. In New Orleans you will really have to search for a DJ spinning the latest top 40, or even the hippest underground indie-rock dance music (you can visit anywhere else and get that, right?). But tons of peeps spin stuff you'll have a hard time describing, and might not hear anywhere else.

DISK JOCKEYS

Beautiful Bells

original ambient; moodgadget.com/beautifulbells

Since 2007, composer, drummer, and producer **Justin Peake** has concocted future jazz from homemade samples and improvised melodies fused with rich sythesized textures. His album *Managing Depth* (Moodgadget) boasts influences as disparate as Fela Kuti, Autechre and John Cage. Catch Beautiful Bells at The Hookah, The Saint or Dragons Den, where Peake plays original tunes more groove-oriented than his exploratory recordings.

Beverly Skillz

hip-hop; beverlyskillz.com

This party DJ spins techno, hip-hop, old skool, 80's music, mash-ups, Baltimore house and more, every Saturday night at **Ohm Lounge** *(135 St. Charles Ave).*

Bomshell Boogie

hip-hop; myspace.com/djbomshell

Another extremely popular DJ and turntablist who packs the **Dragon's Den** at her **Bombshelter** night every Thursday. She specializes in all hip-hop, from abstract and underground to ClearChannel pop.

Brice Nice

everything; bricenice.com

Many claim Brice Nice owns the most records in New Orleans. He also hosts "The Block Party" on 90.7 fm each Saturday 6 to 8 pm, which is designed to fuel an actual blockparty with heavy funk, brass band music, disco, dancehall and other reggae, soul, Afro beat and Latin. Brice also gigs around town, most likely on weekends at The Saint.

Corrosion

goth; corrosion-nola.com

These three Goth music DJs host ambitious dance parties every Sunday at Dragon's Den. Elaborate decorations like bondage gear, black silk, candles, and even metal fencing indoors accentuate sets of both new and classic Goth tunes.

dance in da pants

original instrumental; soundcloud.com/dance-in-da-pants

This live one-man band sings plus plays guitar, bass and keys, frequently collaborating with hip-hop MC **M@ Peoples**.

Rik Ducci

hip-hop; myspace.com/sleptonent

A locally known but nationally respected DJ who has DJed for **KRS-One, EPMD, Busta Rhymes, Lost Boyz, Camp Lo, Naughty by Nature** and the late **Big Pun** among others. Ducci hosts a monthly at **Handsome Willy's** (*218 South Robertson Street*) and a loose weekly at **Le Phare** (*523 Gravier Street*).

Ed Maximillion

hip-hop

Rik Ducci's DJ partner-in-crime. An old school DJ who refuses to bend or fold to the current conditions. He can be found at **Handsome Willy's** on Friday nights or **Le Phare** on Wednesdays providing only the real.

DJ BeesKnees

eclectic; stingingcaterpillar.com/dj-beesknees-stuff

A recovering hip-hop DJ, Beesknees eschews top 40 and now rocks a seamless mix of unusual funk, old and nu-disco, electro, new wave, boogie and Italo. Check the listing in Marigny and Bywater, especially Mimi's.

DJ Chicken

hip-hop;djchicken504.com

Best known these days for the "Chicken and Waffle Mix," drivetime morning show Monday through Friday at 8am on Power 102.9, as well as the throwback lunch mix, DJ Chicken has forever spun old and new hip-hop, bounce rap and brass band music as part of the Definition crew of DJs and MCs.

DJ D Lefty Parker

garage/soul/New Orleans/electro

Parker brings twenty-plus years of expertise as a musician, talent buyer, promoter and record store employee to occasional weeknights spent playing a painstakingly reconstructed MP3 version of his Katrina-ravaged gargantuan record collection for local boozers. Lefty is one of the minds behind the monster rock n'soul revue **Ponderosa Stomp**, and his nights either reflect that event's record-geek aesthetic, or mix of obscure soul, funk, bounce and hip-hop.

DJ Frenzi

....

hip-hop

DJs hip-hop and house DVDs and records simultaneously, most notably on Friday nights at **Omni Royal Orleans Hotel** *(French Quarter,* 621 St Louis St., 504-529-5333).

DJ Jubilee

....

bounce/hip-hop; myspace.com/ djjubilee1

Rapper, DJ, football coach and king of New Orleans "bounce" music for many years now,

Jubilee pops up everywhere from the biggest block parties to **Essence Fest** and **Jazz Fest**. His 90's tracks like "West Bank Thang" and "Do The Jubilee All" are still hot club jams today. He's always hustling; check his Myspace for his most recent residency.

DJ Karo

....

www.deejaykaro.com

With roots in punk and new wave, Karo ended up a hip hop DJ with scratching abilities, who also spins exotic tunes from

The King of New Orleans "bounce" music and hero to the hood, DJ Jubilee.

Bollywood to bounce, to dub reggae with partner **Maddie Ruthless**.

DJ Maddie Ruthless

maddieruthless.com

Know primarily as a reggae and dancehall selector relying mostly on vinyl 45's, Maddie is a musician. As a child she sang in choir and played piano, and eventually moved to London where she fell hard for Rocksteady, a style she infiltrates now as a DJ and singer/songwriter.

DJ Pasta

classic country/undefined; myspace.com/pastapie

Pasta doesn't have a radio show, so you'll have to catch him live – but that's not hard to do, since he spins in a different bar for no cover almost every night. He's the kind of insane record savant who can play four hours' worth of your favorite songs you've never heard of, mostly on 45. Regularly scheduled now, he's got a rock n'roll and punk night, a Louisiana swamp pop night and a weepy country night called **Hangover Tavern**, where if prodded he'll whip out his massive collection of bizarre '60s country novelty songs.

DJ Popppa

www.djpoppa.com

A member of the world-wide Core DJ clique, one of the city's best bounce mixers, and live DJ for bounce artists. Between intermittent spots at Jazz Fest or VooDoo Fest, Poppa holds it down at the Metropolitan (310 Andrew Higgins Dr., 504-568-1702) and House of Blues, which hosts "DJ Poppa's Party House" on Sunday nights.

DJ Proppa Bear

jungle/drum-n-bass; myspace.com/ djproppabear

Now the proprietor of the Dragon's Den – which has been heavy on DJs since he bought the place after Katrina – Proppa spins drum-n-bass and jungle, mostly on Thursdays at his Bass Bin Safari night, which is currently in its tenth year. Novices can come early for an open-mic style vibe, where Proppa gladly passes tricks of the trade onto DJ hopefuls.

DJ Mastadon

Original experimental hip-hop.

DJ Q

Runs tracks for genre-bending bounce rap and dance troupe **NOLA Fam** (see rappers).

DJ Real and Earl the Pearl

hip-hop

This DJ combo creates the penultimate hip-hop party mix at Blue Nile every weekend, late at night till the sun rises, with live drummers and timbales. It gets crazy.

DJs

DJs

E.F. Cuttin

....

hip-hop; efcuttin.com

Member of **Go DJ's**, producer, resident DJ of **Grassroots!** and personal DJ of **Truth Universal**. As a working DJ, E.F. plays to the crowd and breaks quality records on the daily. He heads up the **Industry Influence** parties for Louisiana rap and R&B artists, and also puts together the **Nuthin' But Fire** mixtape series for the record store of the same name. (*see* SHOPPING)

Joey Buttons

....

dance

Spins all vinyl sets of nu disco, old disco, electrofunk and whatever else will make young uptowners dance.

Mr. Cool Bad Guy

....

drum-n-bass/dubstep

Having grown up spinning tribal techno, Patrick Giallombardo found his way to New Orleans in 2007, where he's been a resident DJ for "Bassbin Safari" drum-n-bass night, and cofounded the "Bass Church" Sunday dubstep weekly. He also spins electronic styles including techno/house and breakbeats.

Rusty Lazer

....

bounce; rustylazer.com

If you ever wanted to see white girls get really nasty, Rusty Lazer spins mostly New Orleans bounce music for the punk and fauxbeaux crowds in the Bywater and Marigny neighborhoods. As of late he's also been acting as official DJ for **Big Freedia** (see *Bounce Rap* essay).

N.O. MOMENT:

MOD DANCE PARTY

myspace.com/moddanceparty

A monthly New Orleans tradition for 10 years, the Mod Dance Party – featuring **DJs Kristen**, **Pasta** and **Matt** and their hundreds of pre-1970 vinyl dance records from New Orleans and beyond – is the premier event for those who really like to cut loose and dance to the kind of upbeat 60's soul that the loose moniker 'mod' implies. All music is provided by scratched-up vinyl 45's and LPs – no iPods or laptops allowed. Mod Dance Party was founded by DJ Matty and guitarist/songwriter/music journalist **Michael Hurtt** around Halloween 2000, with the encouragement and prodding of now deceased **Circle Bar** owner **Kelly Keller**, to whom every dance party is dedicated. The party, which routinely goes till dawn (attendance skews young) was more recently moved to the **Saturn Bar** on St. Claude Ave.

in the 9th ward. Their Myspace page features calls for attendees to "Do the Hully-Gully! The Shake! The Twist! The Snake! The **Morgus!** The Sloppy Joe! The Metal Flake Nightmare!" So if that's the sort of thing you like to do, well, this is your spot.

Raj Smoove

hip-hop; rajsmoove.com

This hip-hop and reggae DJ and producer has appeared on **Rap City**, **Showtime at the Apollo**, and **Phat Phat & All That**, to name just a few shows. He's toured with **Cash Money Records, Lil' Wayne,** and **Mannie Fresh**, and has done production for Lil Wayne ("I Miss My Dawgs," "Heat," "Who Wanna"). He hosts Sunday nights at **Metro** *(310 Andrew Higgins)* and at **Club NV** *(1901 Poydras)* every Saturday.

DJ Quickie Mart

hip-hop; djquickiemart.com

After representing the hip-hop/rap in New Orleans for many fruitful years, Quickie Mart recently moved to LA and has become more of a touring national act. Quickie has spun for **Devin the Dude, The Knux**, and the late, great New Orleans MC **Bionik Brown** among many, many others.

DJ Soul Sister

vintage soul; djsoulsister.com

Soul Sister's purview is deep funk, rare groove and disco from the late 60's to early '80s, and she's been known to throw parties that pay specific tribute to **Prince, Michael Jackson**, and early hip-hop. She usually spins two to three times a week live, most often at Mimi's in the Marigny, and between sets at Jazz Fest, Voodoo and Essence. Her long-running *Soul Power* radio show airs from 8 to 10 p.m. Saturday nights on **WWOZ**.

Prince Pauper

reggae

Reggae, dub, dancehall and world music dominate sets by selector Prince Pauper, just as they do his Mid City record store, Domino Sound.

Tony Skratchere

turntablist; tonyskratchere.com

Besides being an intelligent, experienced, in-demand hip-hop DJ, Tony Skratchere – his name a pun on the creole seasoning Tony Chachere's – is the turntablist who invented "Yachtbounce," a new genre that puts a "triggaman" beat behind famous smooht rock songs such as Toto's "Africa." Catch Skratchere anywhere from The Saint to The Dragon's Den to big main event shows at The Republic and VooDoo Fest.

Super Cool DJ Kazu

soul

The regular stand-in when Soul Sister cannot make her Saturday night "Hustle!" party at Mimi's, Kazu spins funk, soul/neo-soul and top 40 pop (the good kind).

DJ NIGHTS AND DANCE CLUBS

Blue Nile

Marigny, 532 Frenchmen St., 504-948-2583; bluenilelive.com

Blue Nile hosts adventurous hip hop duo **DJ Real** and **Earl the Pearl** every weekend, and New Orleans' premier reggae and dancehall selector **DJ T Roy** has a night during the week. On the second Saturday of every month Blue Nile hosts the hip-hop beat battle, Soundclash.

Club Caesar's

West Bank, 209 Monroe St., 504-368-1117

On the other side of the bridge, Caesar's is the place for bounce music, and a regular spot to catch "sissy" bounce artists **Big Freedia, Sissy Nobby** and **Katey Red.**

Chris Owens Club and Balcony

French Quarter, 500 Bourbon St., 504-523-6400; chrisowens.com

One of the last vestiges of the heyday when Bourbon Street was full of wild, original entertainment, Chris Owens is a 60-something showgirl/burlesque dancer who's had so much plastic surgery she looks a bit transsexual. Something's definitely a little off, but that's totally part of the charm. Her club on Bourbon, where she does her singing and dancing act, also hosts salsa dancing and lessons, and hip-hop DJs, as well as some modern top-40 crapola.

Dragon's Den

Marigny, 435 Esplanade Ave., 504-949-1750; myspace.com/dragonsdennola

After the flood, **DJ Proppa Bear** bought the Den and installed turntables both upstairs and downstairs, where a second stage was also added. Electronic music parties featuring hip-hop, jungle, reggaeton and the like, were added to the club's already perfectly eclectic roster of rock, brass bands, and every other music in between.

The Duck Off

Gentilly, 2304 A P Tureaud Ave., 504-947-3633; myspace.com/theduckoff

Located in Gentilly, a flooded neighborhood not detailed elsewhere in this book, The Duck Off – as you will quickly learn if you listen to local hip-hop station **Q93.3 FM** for even a minute – is the only club in New Orleans with its own ringtone. Their regular DJ, **Money Fresh**, also curates mixtapes of local rap remixes and originals under the club's imprimatur. Stop by Sunday late-afternoon, when a brass band is usually throwing down with a rapper or two. It's an awesome spot to check out the real-deal local hip-hop scene, but tourists should use street smarts and caution; it is

in the 'hood, so park close, and don't be a jerk.

Handsome Willy's (bar)

CBD, 218 S. Robertson St, 504-525-0377; handsomewillys.com

One of the only cool places to hang out in the CBD, with live DJs, dance parties, and many many free BBQs and crab boils. Located in the medical area of the CBD near the arena and **Super Dome**, Willy's is closed Sundays unless the **Saints** are in the Dome.

Hostel Restaurant & Ultra-Lounge

French Quarter, 329 Decatur St. , 504-587-0036; hostelnola.com

A sort of upscale restaurant with live DJs spinning modern tunes. Of course where DJs show up, so will rappers, so now there are intelligent, professional rap shows at this opulent yet comfortable venue for dining, entertainment and special events.

Howlin' Wolf

CBD/Warehouse District, 907 S Peters St., 504-529-5844; howlin-wolf.com

The Wolf is a hard place to pin down. Once a major contender in the city, its status has been significantly shrunk over the years by House of Blues who, with Clear Channel money behind them, can outbid any truly local club. But The Wolf has its faults too, being just one big not very charming room,

DJs

with nowhere to go but outside for any kind of break (thank God you can drink outside here!). But the sound is pristine, and the dude who owns it has been championing the local scene forever.

LePhare

523 Gravier St., 504-636-1891; lepharenola.com

This upscale lounge seems a little stuffy but hosts hip-hop and other DJs multiple nights a week.

Platinum 3000

Mid-City, 2201 Banks St., 504-324-4187; myspace.com/clubunlimited

Another hip-hop club with a concentration in bounce music; another good spot to check out "sissy" bounce artists.

R Bar

Marigny, 1431 Royal St., 504-948-7499; royalstreetinn.com

R Bar is now owned in part by former **Afghan Whigs** frontman and current **Twilight Singer** and **Gutter Twin, Greg Dulli**. For info on the R Bar's **Royal Street Inn**, see *Hotels.*

The Saint

961 St. Mary St; 504-523-0050; defendneworleans.com

As close as New Orleans ever gets to hipsterism, this truly great bar was recently sold by the bassist from **White Zombie** to the owner of the popular

Bartender Skwirl at The Saint, which hosts tons of DJs.

DAN FOX

Defend New Orleans clothing line. An ultra late-night, often rowdy bar (the photo booth has immortalized some of the most debauched moments in New Orleans drinking), The Saint hosts DJ and dance parties as often as possible. Sunday nights are a mainstay with **DJ** **Pasta's** tear-in-your-beer country night, **Hangover Tavern**. Other nights feature everything from aggressive metal to booty bass; check the web for up-to-date listings.

N.O. MOMENT:

DRUMCART

You'll understand why it's spelled in all caps after you see/ hear/feel DRUMCART roll through the scene: three drum kits attached to a mobile cart, combining the heaviness of **Black Sabbath** and the danceability of **Michael Jackson**. From the center sprouts a tall chair from which a costumed hype-person revs the crowd. (*myspace.com/noladrumcart*)

RADIO STATIONS

DJ Bombshell Boogie

JT

WTUL 91.5FM

eclectic modern; wtulneworleans.com

Tulane University's legendary radio station is one of the best in town, spinning anything and everything from indie rock to hip-hop, metal, squalling punk and vintage country, with requisite attention to all local bands working outside the brass/jazz/funk box – WTUL plays **Quintron and Miss Pussycat** multiple times a day. WTUL also publish the satiric but musically informative coffeeshop zine *The Vox.*

WWOZ 90.7FM

New Orleans/world/roots; wwoz.org

New Orleans' community radio station started more than a quarter century ago in a studio above **Tipitina's** uptown; after getting rained out of their Armstrong Park studio by Katrina, they're currently in the French Quarter. OZ routinely wins all sorts of awards, and is an icon for roots and jazz fans worldwide, who listen on their streaming webcast With a 24-hour schedule of volunteer show hosts, all kinds of weirdness can happen; listen in the early mornings for trad jazz and New Orleans music, and afternoon and early evening for blues and R&B. For real on-air weirdness, listen after 10 p.m., when undersupervised hosts will spin everything from **Ennio Morricone** to **Sun Ra** to tapes of the late legendary oddball **Ernie K-Doe** hosting his show in the '90s. Once, I heard two DJs energetically comparing strains of weed that had competed in that year's Amsterdam Cannabis Cup over a marathon playlist of obscure **James Booker** tapes.

WQUE 93.3 FM

New Orleans' longest-running hip-hop and R&B station is owned by Clear Channel, but has little of that corporate monster's blandness: in fact, its programming has tons of local flavor. Weekday afternoon DJ Wild Wayne is a local legend, and his Sunday night (7-9 p.m.) "504 Radio" show features all old-school New Orleans hip-hop. Listening to Q93 is also the best way to stay hip to upcoming rap shows around town.

POWER 102.9

modern urban; power1029.com

For fans of modern Black music, a good alternative to the highly repetitive local Clear Channel "urban top-40" format, 102.9 has actual human DJs curating their own shows. **Mike Swift** airs weekly from 2 to 7pm (with an hour break at 5pm), and Saturday 10am to 2pm. You'll still definitely get your **Beyonce,** but she may come sandwiched between **MOS DEF** and **Common.**

DJs

Some round-the-way girls outside a concert by popular "sissy bounce" rappers, Big Freedia and Sissy Nobby.

RESTAURANTS THAT FEATURE
MUSIC AND/OR ART

Your vacation and its menu of artistic stimulation doesn't have to stop when you sit down to eat! Many New Orleans restaurants feature music and/or rotating art exhibits, while others are attached to music venues or are open late night for post-concert chow-down.

Le Bon Temps Roulé, a famous brass band club that serves serviceable bar food plus FREE oysters on Fridays at happy hour, was at one point owned by Corrosion of Conformity and Down guitarist, Pepper Keenan.

3 Muses

Marigny, 536 Frenchmen St. , 504-252-4801; thethreemuses.com

With music every night plus constantly rotating art and photography exhibits, plus delicious, creative bar food, Three Muses brings together middle class folks in a tasteful, unique, smoke free environment. Hospitality specialist **Sophie Lee** is also a passable torch singer, relaying a sultry blend of jazz and swing ala Ella Fitzgerald and Billie Holiday.

Checkpoint Charlie's

Marigny, 501 Esplanade Ave., 504-281-4847; myspace.com/checkpoints

Checkpoints is one of several pubs around town all owned by a man named Igor that all feature 24-hour booze, food, laundry, pinball, pool, wi-fi and video games, plus free red beans and sausage every Monday night. Straddling the Quarter and the Marigny at the mouth of the Frenchmen Street strip, Checkpoint's also hosts live music nightly: everything from obnoxious punk bands to open-mike blues jams. Sometimes an out-of-towner headlines, but otherwise it's the 3 a.m. spot in which to listen to a local singer-songwriter and eat a cheeseburger while doing your laundry.

Coop's

French Quarter, 1109 Decatur St., 504-525-9053; coopsplace.net

Coop's doesn't host live music, but being just a short stumble from Frenchmen Street or **One Eyed Jacks**, it's the perfect late-night post-concert spot, with arguably the best non-touristy Cajun and Creole inflected food in the Quarter. On into the morning, Coop's serves consistent fried oysters and shrimp, crab claws, redfish, plus gumbo, etouffee, and a rabbit and sausage jambalaya so good it will make you eat bunny. The fried chicken is spicy, the red beans and rice are porky, and specialties like the smoked-duck quesadilla and chicken Tchoupitoulas with shrimp, tasso and bacony green beans, go above and beyond the call of soaking up booze.

Howling Wolf Den

Uptown, 907 S. Peters St., 504-529-5844; thehowlinwolf.com/the-den

Attached to the much bigger Howling Wolf, the den handles smaller acts, including the **Soundclash** Beat Battle. In the club's frontroom you can mow on sandwiches, plus New Orleansy bar appetizers like fried pickles, crawfish aies, meat pies, gator, chicken jamabalya and much more.

Jacques-Imo's

Uptown, 8324 Oak St., 504-861-0886; jacquesimoscafe.com

Jacques-Imo's is sort of a musical work of funky art in itself, attached as it is to the famed **Maple Leaf** music club.

FOOD

It's not unheard of for the entire **Rebirth Brass Band** (who've played the Leaf every Tuesday for forever) to parade over from next door and blast the restaurant with horns and thumping drums for at least two courses' length. The wacky chef is a local personality (a mural of him in his signature Iams chef pants graces the side of the building) and his food is an unpretentious, skillfully done Creole soul-food that does the traditional favorites (barbecue shrimp and corn maqué choux) but doesn't do them to death (acorn squash stuffed with mussels in curry cream).

Juan's Flying Burrito

Uptown, 2018 Magazine St., 504-569-0000; 4724 S Carrollton Ave, 504-486-9950; juansflyingburrito.com

In the tradition of Austin or San Francisco, Juan's is the Tex-Mex dive of New Orleans, featuring over-stuffed burritos, nachos, tacos, a full service bar and a tatted-up staff that's practically a gang. They pick the music: usually Black Sabbath, or else one of their own bands. Despite the blare of **Eyehategod** or **Suplecs**, you'll find everyone from business folk and doctors to the rockerati of New Orleans happily downing potent margaritas. Juan's also features a revolving display of artwork with the same punk/pierced theme.

La Peniche

Marigny, 1940 Dauphine St., 504-943-1460

Where other cities have Denny's, Perkins, or other corporate brands, we have La Peniche, serving simultaneous breakfast, lunch and dinner–plus homemade desserts!–until the morning. They're open around the clock from Friday night till Sunday morning and late-night every other day, just a two-block stumble from Frenchmen's music scene.

Le Bon Temps Roule

Uptown, 4801 Magazine St., 504-897-3448; myspace.com/4801magazine

This down-home fun Uptown funk and brass band bar (see the Music Clubs sections) serves pub grub and sandwiches, with free oysters on Fridays.

Liuzza's by the Track

Mid-City, 1518 N. Lopez St., 504-218-7888

Amazing bloody marys, non-traditional but supreme gumbo, and the best Reuben ever. The restaurant is located just outside the busy mouth of Jazzfest, though at that time they batten down the hatches, and serve a faster, truncated menu on paper plates. Everything is still good, but we suggest going down for dinner early on Thursday night so you can stick around for Liuzza's traditional impromptu acoustic bluegrass night, where banjos, fiddles, and stand-up basses abound in stringy, twangy casual glory.

Clint Maedgen performs at Mimi's in the Marigny with adventurous cellist Helen Gillet.

Michaul's

....

Central Business District, 840 St. Charles Ave., 504-522-5517; michauls.com

Don't let our "underground" theme make you think we don't relish the original traditions of New Orleans, which are still fun and alive in some corners of the city. Michaul's has great, cheap New Orleans food and drinks, plus live Cajun and zydeco music. It's as Cajun as you can get here in *la ville*. The waitresses even teach customers to Cajun line dance. Michaul's big picture window looks right out onto the streetcar line, and grand Lee Circle a little ways up. For Mardi Gras, Michaul's sells reasonably-priced wristbands that entitle the wearer to buffet food, drinks, and a nice bathroom (because as **Benny Grunch's** famous local song goes, "Ain't no place to pee on Mardi Gras day!")

Mimi's in the Marigny

....

Marigny, 2601 Royal St., 504-872-9868 mimisinthemarigny.com

Late-night boozing and music does not have to mean cheese fries and jalapeno poppers. One of the city's most popular bars, Mimi's, offers a sexy-bohemian vibe and a delicious Castilian menu of hot and cold tapas mostly under $8 each, served till four a.m., with a very decent wine list to boot. Upstairs the local art exhibits rotate monthly, and the bands play nightly. Intimate shows runs the gamut from gypsy-folk circus-type acts, famous local artists' side-project experiments, amazing country cover bands, smart DJs, and other musical oddities that suit the cozy space. No cover.

Siberia

Marigny, 2227 St Claude Ave., 265-8855

While listening to heavy rock of some sort, eat thoughtful late-night bar food, every dish under $10, all designed and served up by **Heath Hailey**, creator of the outstanding tapas kitchen at Mimi's in the Marigny. The fish-n-chips are proper. The bison burger is for true carnivores only.

Sports Vue Tavern

Marigny, 1701 Elysian Fields Ave., 504-940-1111

In the dwindling New Orleans tradition of daiquiri shop as African-American meeting ground (ala the babershop everywhere else in America) this non-smoking ultra-hangout has pizza and other

tables and, on not infrequent occasions, live New Orleans bounce rap. Truly special drink specials and a chance to rub elbows with very real locals.

St. Roch Tavern

Marigny/St. Roch, 1200 Saint Roch Ave., 504-208-6582

This is a divey bar with food at the edge of Treme–close enough to walk from the Marigny and Quarter, but you shouldn't. It's big-ish inside, warmly lit, cheap and dirty, but cozy, and near a couple of funky, community-run art spaces (**Homespace** and **Sidearm**). Meaning, it is indeed a block you could hang out on all evening, as long as you don't stray from where people can see you. Everything from punk bands to blues acts play any night of the week, and on weekend DJ nights, the grassroots-activist bicycle crowd

Hip folks at Mimi's in the Marigny.

ROBIN WALKER

bar food to munch while partaking of many arcade games, electronic basketball and darts, mad pool

dances to Baltimore club music, Miami booty bass and NOLA bounce (Sound incongruous?

That's New Orleans). There's a recently opened kitchen in the back, serving a variety of sandwiches and other superior bar foods.

Star Steak and Lobster

French Quarter, 237 Decatur St., 504-525-6151; starsteak.com

The food here is good enough, but the real treat while eating steak, lobster, crab cakes and grilled oysters is one-man-band **James Dee** (Wed. through Sun., 6 to 10pm), who with his truly original music, plus his pompadour, reverb-heavy saxophone, Casio keyboard beats and dramatic but mellow voice, will never leave your memory of New Orleans – imagine Tom Waits as a cruise ship entertainer. "**Famous Joey**," has also served as Star's doorman for over 29 years.

Sweet Lorraine's Jazz Club

Marigny, 1931 St. Claude Ave., 504-945-9654; sweetlorrainesjazzclub.com

From the outside, it looks like a dive bar, but Sweet Lorraine's is stunningly decorated on the inside and features live jazz music on weekday nights, ranging from **Michael Ward** to one **Marsalis** or another. Their menu includes seafood, pasta dishes, and New Orleans specialties like jambalaya and po-boys. Sunday afternoons Sweet Lorraine's cooks up their $25 Jazz Brunch buffet, featuring live music.

FOOD

St. Roch Tavern, a charmingly unsafe, surprisingly good place for live music and bar food.

ZS

FOOD

N.O. MOMENT:

THE OFFICIAL SNACKS OF NEW ORLEANS

Zapp's are the official (and officially perfect) potato chips of New Orleans. Our beer is the flavorful **Abita Beer** (which comes in all types from Christmas Ale to a satsuma-flavored brew) while kids and adults enjoy **Barq's Root Beer**, or **Big Shot** red drink. Our fried snack desserts are called **Hubig's Pies** (from lemon to chocolate to peach to sweet potato). **Boiled shrimp** are also a decadent (and messy) snack, as are **boiled crawfish**; sniff around and you'll find a bar serving up the crustaceans for free at happy hour. During summer, a giant Styrofoam cup full of frozen daiquiri to-go from one of our many local **daiquiri** stands (we suggest **Gene's**, the big pink building in Marigny, on St. Claude and Elysian Fields,) will save your life, especially if you're on a bike. During Mardi Gras there is also **King Cake** to be scarfed, but if your piece (or one of your pieces) has a lil' plastic baby hidden in it, then assuming you don't choke, you must buy the next King Cake. Sorry, them's the rules.

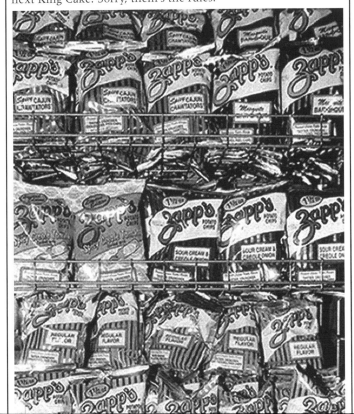

Vaughan's

....

Bywater; 4229 Dauphine St., 504-947-5562

Everyone from **The Rolling Stones** to **Will Oldham** have made the trek all the mildly intimidating way back into the Bywater hood to visit Vaughan's, the most famous bar you'd probably miss on a visit to New Orleans. Every Thursday night for roughly 20 years, Vaughan's has hosted some form of brass dance music, mostly **Kermit Ruffins**, an unoriginal but very fun trumpet player (think Louis Armstrong with a heavier marijuana emphasis – see the Music Clubs section). Since the Uptown college kids discovered Vaughan's (Thursdays are the only nights you'll see taxis in Bywater) Thursday night's cover has gone up to $10 and they only serve the beans. The rest of the week Vaughan's stays purely local, and you're guaranteed to meet someone nice and funny to talk and sip with. Outside of Thursdays, the bar is extremely generous with food, including free boiled seafood on Friday nights, and amazing spreads during Saints games and every other New Orleans holiday.

FOOD

House of a Thousand Hertz recording studio owner and personal soundman to sax god Maceo Parker, Goat (aka Andrew Gilchrist) poses with a real goat outside Vaughan's bar in Bywater.

OTHER NEW ORLEANS FOODS: MORE FOODS THAT NEW ORLEANS DOES REAL WELL

Trying to eat healthy while on vacation and still eat New Orleans-y food? Well, lucky for you the city hosts a huge Vietnamese population, concentrated in a 'Little Vietnam' out in New Orleans East (not very far–just take Chef Menteur Highway east until you see the all Vietnamese strip malls on your left). New Orleans West Bank on the other side of the Mississippi River, is also a haven for excellent Asian chefs. Beyond Vietnamese, New Orleans hosts every Asian possibility from cheap buffets to high-priced sushi. In fact, Asian cultures have so influenced New Orleans that many of our rickety corner stores and gas stations sell fried rice dishes with their po-boys, and crawfish pies alongside (often amazing) egg rolls. (Special thanks to local Jack Porobil for his expertise):

ASIAN / VIETNAMESE

Pho yo tastebuds.

DAN FOX

China Wall Restaurant

....

Chinese, CBD, 1112 Canal St., 504-522-6802

This good-enough Chinese place is most remarkable for the fact that they deliver all the way back into Bywater. A killer order of mushu pork (more than enough for two people) and ten big crab rangoons costs about $15.

Hong Kong Food Market

All Asian, Westbank,
925 Behrman Hwy., 504-394-7075

A super local mega mart of fresh Asian food ingredients, with a concentration on Vietnamese. Incredible produce, live seafood tanks, a deli, plus a Vietnamese restaurant area serving everything from pho to Vietnamese po-boys.

King Buffet

All Asian, Metairie,
601 Veterans Memorial Blvd.,
504-837-4383; kingbuffet.net

There are tons of these comprehensive Asian buffets all over America. King Buffet out in Metairie is the best one we've found locally. The sushi is replenished a little more often than at other places, plus the crab rangoons are awesome, *and* they serve sake. $10

Lost Love Lounge / Pho King

Vietnamese; Marigny, 2529
Dauphine St.; 504-400-6145

This charming and familial new dive bar up the street from Mimi's is not only owned in part by banjo/guitar dude Geoff Douville from Egg Yolk Jubilee, but they also host (Thurs. through Sun., 6pm to late-night) a great Vietnamese restaurant in the back called Marigny Pho.

Nine Roses

Vietnamese/Chinese, Gretna on the
Westbank, 1100 Stephen St.,
504-366-7665

A nice place but very affordable. The dishes wherein you grill beef, shrimp and/or chicken at your table yourself, then wrap in rice paper, easily feeds two to three people for around $15.

Mikimoto Japanese Restaurant

Japanese, 3301 S. Carrollton Ave.,
504.488.1881; mikimotosushi.com

This very basic, small sushi restaurant has tons of great one-dollar sashimi and roll specials. They also have a drive-thru window for pickup, or if you want to avoid your car altogether, they offer the fastest delivery known to man.

Pho Tau Bay

Vietnamese, Gretna, just off the
Westbank Expwy., Stumpf exit, 113
504-368-9846

Specializing in pho (rice noodles, pork, mint, shrimp, bean sprouts, meat,) Pho Tau Bay also serves amazing fresh springrolls, as well as Vietnamese style iced coffee: New Orleans chicory coffee French-dripped over condensed milk, to be mixed up and poured over ice. The drink's French-Asian roots make it perfect for New Orleans, especially in the summer.

Pho Bang

Vietnamese, Metairie, 8814
Veterans Memorial Blvd.,
504-466-8742

Pho Bang serves pho and other Vietnamese soups almost exclusively. Pho is served a number of ways: tendon, tripe, beef balls, fresh eye of round, brisket, navel...you can get pretty much any part of the cow or pig in your bowl.

Sake Cafe

....

Uptown, 2830 Magazine St.
504-894-0033

A little expensive, but you can't put a price on this kind of artistry. Given that Sake Café's original New Orleans-ified rolls and other seafood dishes are delicious works of art – plus the restaurant's modern décor, too, is intriguing and creative – you might expect it all to cost even more.

Sukho Thai

....

Marigny, 1913 Royal St.,
504-948-9309

One of the only upscale-ish non-sushi Asian restaurants inside the city proper. Tasty enough Thai curries and noodles, though the portions aren't as big as the prices.

Wasabi Sushi Restaurant & Bar

....

Marigny, 900 Frenchmen St.,
504-943-9433

A simple mid-range sushi restaurant that nonetheless has the power to get you high off their fresh fish concoctions, and nice selection of sakes. We've had more than one meal here where we walked away agreeing that we'd just had the best sushi of our lives. If we could recommend only one sushi restaurant in the city, Wasabi is definitely it.

CRAWFISH

You can get this boiled spicy poor-man's shrimp all year round somewhere in the city, but you will pay dearly, and they'll be puny. Crawfish are biggest and best during the chillier months – coincidentally or not, all through New Orleans' festival season. We protest anything above $2 a pound. Here are some other crawdaddy options:

ZS

Our photographer Zack Smith and friends at a very real crawfish "berl."

Captain Sal's Seafood and Chicken

Bywater, 3168 Saint Claude Ave.
504-948-9990

If you're in Bywater / Marigny, Captain Sal's is the place. A big hot deli counter with everything from egg rolls to crawfish pies to boiled shrimp and soft-shelled crabs. Grab a cheap beer and sit down, cover the dirty table with newspaper, dump out the crawdads, figure out how to crack `em open, get into the rhythm, stare out the window onto crazy-ass St. Claude Ave., and you just may understand New Orleans.

Big Fisherman

Uptown, 3301 Magazine St.,
504-897-9907

Kind of expensive for crawfish but Big Fisherman certainly know what they doin' in regards to spice.

K-Jean Seafood

Mid-City 236 N Carrollton Ave.,
504-488-7503

Charming little Mid-City shack that rebuilt and rebounded strong after Katrina. Hard working crawfish experts, these people.

DAIQUIRIS

Daiquiri stands are another option which locals utilize daily. During New Orleans' hot summer, especially if you're riding your bike, a frozen daiquiri to-go can save your life. Though several honest-to-god drive-thru daiquiri stands still exist on the Westbank and in other suburbs (the drive-thru worker hands it down into your car, with the straw sitting across the lid; only if you drove off and poked the straw down in could you be busted for DUI), drive-thrus unfortunately went extinct inside New Orleans proper after Katrina. French Quarter daiquiris do taste good, but they're hella expensive (a medium, enough for a good buzz, should cost less than $6), and they're never as potent. Find yourself a good generous neighborhood daiquiri stand, and the only thing you'll have to worry about is drinking just one (WARNING: drink one early in the day and you may survive till nighttime, maybe, but if you drink two, between the alcohol and the sugar you will surely crash hard before sundown). Man, do we love daiquiris though.

Gene's Po-Boys and Daiquiris

Marigny, 1040 Elysian Fields Ave.,
504-943-3861

In the hood, this is the spot. Bounce music on the radio, video poker in back, an extra sweet older lady workin the counter, and frozen to-go drinks. Make sure and ask to see the menu, featuring crazily-named daiquiri combos made up by the neighborhood such as The Good Joog, What the Fuck, Slim Shady (all the white liquors), and our favorite, Sweet Pussy (peach mixed with white Russian).

Daiquiri Place Cafe

....

1401 Saint Charles Ave.,
504-524-1401

Many consider this the best daiquiri stand in the city, with drinks made from actual fruit that are just strong enough. Right off of Lee Circle, amid lots of nice tony restaurants and bars, Daiquiri Place Cafe is a deeply local hangout where you're as certain to meet some natives as you are to have some frozen drinks.

New Orleans Original Daiquiris

....

10 locations; 504-524-9504

The local chain. Better than nothing, and in a pinch, still excellent for chillin' outside somewhere. If you really want a buzz you'll have to pay a buck for an extra shot.

FOOD

ICE CREAM

Angelo Brocato Ice Cream

....

Mid-City, 214 N Carrollton
Ave., 50-486-0078;
angelobrocatoicecream.com

This Italian ice cream hot spot is old-fashioned and thoroughly local. Besides incredible ice cream, Brocato's has gelato, canolis, fresh dessert pastries, and tables so you can sit down and focus on the best dessert experience in the city.

The Creole Creamery

....

Uptown, 4924 Prytania St., 504-
894-8680; creolecreamery.com

This kid-friendly "ice cream experience" specializes in unique flavors, from Carmel Chicory Chocolate, to Cucumber Sorbet. The street it's on, Prytania, is a great shopping and restaurant street.

La Divina Gelateria

....

Uptown and *French Quarter, 3005*
Magazine St., 504-342-2634, and
621 St. Peter St., 504-302-2692;
ladivinagelateria.com

Written up in the *New York Post* for the quality of its gelato, La Divina use all locally sourced ingredients, from berries to cream, and old-school Italian methods to churn out the icy goodness. They also serve a lunch menu of salads and panini, plus espresso drinks. A French Quarter satellite recently opened near Jackson Square.

INDIAN FOOD

Hare Krishna House (free, vegan)

....

2936 Esplanade Ave., 504-304-0032; myspace.com/iskcon_nola

Every Sunday these Krishnas host a free Indian food meal. A "Love Feast" to be exact, on Sunday evenings, with *kirtan* beginning at 5:30pm, followed by a special *arati* at 6, a discourse from 6:45 to 7:30pm, then the aforementioned Krishna *prasadam* (spiritual food) served free of charge to everyone. We wouldn't suggest you go here and eat great free vegan Indian food if you were going to be set upon by cultists; New Orleans' Krishnas are mostly non-American, very kind and sweet, and not the least bit pushy, making this a great casual environment in which to check out a different way of life while having good food – a bit of a ritual for New Orleanians who are low on cash and want some healthy dining. Plus, it's a very pretty early-evening bike ride down Esplanade Ave.

Nirvana Indian Cuisine

....

4308 Magazine St., 504-894-9797; insidenirvana.com

The only place within the city proper that hosts an Indian lunch buffet daily, plus dinner buffet on Thursday and Sunday.

PIZZA

Not sure why you're eating pizza on your visit to New Orleans but… Pizza in New Orleans is really meant to be eaten by the slice from various windows during Mardi Gras, or all year round anywhere near Bourbon Street. But if you really need a whole pie (and we certainly understand that need), here are our suggestions:

Bywater Resturant & Deli

....

Bywater, 3162 Dauphine St., 504-944-4445

For pizza in Bywater, this is your only hope. Order it or dine-in at this charming restaurant with its fun funky art, great courtyard, tasty drinks and dynamic array of food choices – from gumbo to ribs to brisket to salads to ruebens.

Slice

....

Uptown, 1513 St. Charles Ave., 504-525-PIES); slicepizzeria.com

The yin to **Juan's Flying Burrito's** yang, Slice is run by the same people, though it doesn't quite follow the hardcore aesthetic of its older brother. Whether pizza by the slice or a whole pie, Slice offers better fare than most of the city's pizza joints, including special salads and small plates.

PO-BOYS

The po-boy is a simple thing. Fried seafood or else meat on French bread, "dressed," if you like, with mayo, tomato, and lettuce, maybe some pickles. No more. No mustard even. Given its simplicity – plus the fact that New Orleans does all food so right – most po-boys you'll eat in New Orleans will be pretty damn good. Long as the bread is crunchy, the shrimp medium sized, and afterwards you're stuffed and there are still a few shrimp/oysters/ hunks of roast beef left on the big white butcher paper, then that's a wrap Out of thousands of good po-boy joints, these are just the first three that come to mind:

FOOD

Coop's Place

French Quarter, 1109 Decatur St., 504-525-9053; coopsplace.net

We'd like to tell you only about on-the-corner down-low po-boy joints, but if you're in the Quarter and want New Orleans food late into the night, Coop's is the absolute best, even though it's popular. Coop's is consistently hoppin, and loud. Big fat fried oysters on French bread or a bun are sublime, but we also love the blackened redfish po-boy.

Magnolia Discount

Midcity; 1233 N. Broad St., 504-486-0086

A not remarkably clean gas station that can nonetheless blow your mind with over-*over*-stuffed shrimp and other 16-inch po-boys. Meaning, roughly two giant meals for less than $10. Again, you can pop in most gas stations that sell po-boys (earlier in the day the better as far as French bread goes), and probably end up with a good deal.

Parkway Bakery

Mid-City, 538 Hagan Avenue, 504-482-2680; parkwaybakeryandtavernnola.com

Considered by many po-boy experts to have the absolute best roast beef po-boy smothered in "debris" gravy that you could possibly ever have – ever. Parkway is also a very nice family bar with a view of the water on Bayou St. John, just outside City Park.

Parasol's Restaurant & Bar

Uptown, 2533 Constance Street; 504-899-2054; parasols.com

Part dive-bar, part poboy shop, part community center, Parasol's is the anchor of the Irish Channel neighborhood and is a great place to catch a football game and an oyster poboy. It is also the epicenter of all St. Patrick's Day activities. 7 days, 12pm-til

COFFEE SHOPS

Almost all of the following independently-owned coffee shops also host live local music. If not, we included them for some other damn good reason.

Lil Doogie, the puppet alter-ego of local comedy-rapper Ballzack, is huge on YouTube for his New Orleans inside jokes. Also he drinks tea.

Café DuMonde

French Quarter, 800 Decatur St., 1-800-772-2927; cafedumonde.com

Every visiting tourist has to stop in the outside courtyard of Café DuMonde, across from beautiful Jackson Square, for the only thing they serve: fried and powdered beignets and chicory coffee (a wonderfully rich, almost dirty-tasting New Orleans version of joe). The live musicians who play to the courtyard for tips will never let you forget you're a tourist. Still, we are not snobby enough to guide you away from this wonderful experience.

DAN FOX

A band plays outside Cafe Du Monde in the Quarter.

Byrdie's

Bywater, 2422A St. Claude Ave.,
656-6794; byrdiesgallery.com

This tea and coffee shop, which features sandwiches and other lunch fare, doubles as an official SCAD art gallery and as a ceramics studio that offers classes as well as memberships for those just needing a kiln. A new gallery show opens on the second Saturday night of each month.

Café Envie

French Quarter, 1241 Decatur St.,
504-524-3689; myspace.com/envienola

When you imagine sitting in a coffee shop in New Orleans – or France for that matter – idly sipping espresso while watching the world go buy, you are picturing Envie. This open-air café is perfectly situated on lower Decatur for tourists who'd like to hang with locals, and have something to look at out the many open French doors. The young baristas double as competent DJs, their iPods piping in all decades of college rock music.

Café Rose Nicaud

Marigny, 632 Frenchmen St.,
504-949-3300

During the day, before the live music starts, Frenchmen is still a neighborhood hub for locals, and Rose Nicaud, which bookends the Royal Street end of the strip, is a popular spot for coffee, laptop work, and lazing with a newspaper by the big picture windows. Though the prices are not small and the portions aren't big, Rose Nicaud does offer food, plus live New Orleans music on weekends and other special occasions.

Croissant d'Or

French Quarter, 617 Ursulines St.,
504-524-4663

No music here but everything else more than compensates. This airy bakery, with its azure walls, white tile and flooding sunlight, evokes casual Euro chic à la the South of France. Homemade French pastries are sweet or savory, and the baguettes are golden, chewy and light. Oh – and really cheap. Beware though: they close at 2:30 p.m.

Fair Grinds

Mid-City, 3133 Ponce Deleon St.,
504-913-9072; fairgrinds.com

In the extra room upstairs, Fair Grinds hosts everything from art films to yoga to book releases to folk music to potluck dinners to mellow, avant-garde noise concerts. Right down the sidewalk from the cemetery, the **New Orleans Museum of Art**, and **Liuzza's by the Track**, not to mention the **New Orleans Fair Grounds** (get it?) home of Jazz Fest.

Flora's coffee shop in Bywater rents computers to bums without laptops.

Flora Gallery & Coffee Shop

....

Marigny, 2600 Royal St., New Orleans; 947-8358

No live music, but tons of musicians. Flora's is New Orleans' quintessential bohemian coffeeshop – located on a great little local corner of bars and restaurants – which features tons of interesting fliers and other local ads tacked to its door, plus rentable desktop computers for those without laptops. There's almost always someone strumming an instrument on the benches outside next to grizzled old hippies playing chess. Flora's coffee drinks are cheaper than their Mediterranean and breakfast foods. And Flora's smells much nicer now that you can't smoke inside.

JuJu Bag

....

Gentilly neighborhood [north of Marigny,] 4706 Mandeville St., 504-872-0969

The JuJu Bag Café, with its huge sun deck out back, supports and hosts many community events including a weekly poetry night, book signings, Sunday brunch, plus meetings and receptions.

Orange Couch

....

Marigny, 2339 Royal Street; 267-7327 theorangecouchcoffee.com

An upscale yet still comfy coffeeshop located on a funky corner in the Marigny. Fancy coffees are served beside light Vietnamese dishes and mochi Japanese ice cream rice balls. Orange Couch shows local artists and photographers, and sometimes hosts community performances, such as students from nearby **NOCCA** performing arts school.

FOOD

Rue De La Course

....

Uptown, at 3121 Magazine St. and various other locations,
504-899-0242

A local chain that's hardly chain-y, Rue's flagship outpost is smack in the middle of the Magazine Street shopping strip, with another Uptown on the up-and-coming Oak Street strip. Both serve coffee and espresso drinks, pastries and sandwiches all day. The large windows, green-shaded work lamps, dark wood tables and chairs and large chalkboards create a sort of old-New-Orleans/old Europe vibe, and both shops are popular with students and other patrons who park for hours with their laptops. The atmosphere is both regal and relaxed, and while the service can be a little off-putting at times (earning it the nickname "Rude, Of Course") it's all part of the charm.

Sound Café / Beth's Books

....

Marigny, 2700 Chartres St.,
504-947-4477

Sound Café is a pleasant little respite of a coffee shop near the Press Street tracks (the border between Bywater and Marigny), where locals sit with laptops,

Uptown people-watching spot Rue De La Course coffee shop, amidst many cool clothing shops, is a haven for hipsters and nursing and law students with laptops.

coffee, sandwiches and pastries. The café hosts intermittent concerts by brass bands and other lively acoustic music, and at any given time local musicians (who rarely work during the day) might jump on the piano in the corner and practice for the clientele. The café shares the building with **Beth's Books**, specializing in high-quality used books, plus tons of titles by New Orleans authors.

St. Coffee
....
Marigny, 2709 St Claude Ave; 872-9798

Serves up the usual coffeehouse stuff, plus Jarritos Mexican sodas, excellent doughnuts and fresh pastries.

Z'otz
....
Uptown, 8210 Oak St., 504-861-2224; myspace.com/zotzcoffee

Named for a Mayan glyph, Z'otz's sign doesn't bear its name – just a giant question mark. Still, it's hard to miss. The 24-hour shop is big with students, Goth kids and bohemian sorts who enjoy the unusual candies, vegan pastries and unique offerings like bubble tea and yerba mate. Their semi-regular "night market" – an after-dark crafts bazaar – is popular, as are occasional DJ nights, open-mic events, and acoustic performances.

FOOD

Beth's Books next to Sound Cafe Coffee shop on the corner of Port St. and Chartres in Marigny

MARDI GRAS SEASON:

A MONTH OF LOVE AND PARTIES

*There is just too much one can say about **Fat Tuesday**, and the month-plus of parades and parties and concerts that precedes it (**Twelfth Night**, or the Epiphany, is the official start of Carnival season). The party peaks the night before Fat Tuesday, which is called **Lundi Gras**. Mardi Gras day is really the drunken, still-ecstatic wind-down to the world's longest debauch. You didn't know that? Well, there's probably a lot you don't know about Mardi Gras.*

Whether you've visited New Orleans or not (especially if you haven't!), close your eyes for a moment and picture Mardi Gras. Now, know that

The Secret Society of St. Anne Parade. Notice there are no spectators, only costumed participants.

whatever you pictured is certainly going on somewhere in the city, but so is every other celebratory thing you could dream up. Sure, you could lick hurricane drink off a stranger's bare breast on a busy street. But you could also likely have a quiet crawfish picnic with Mormons if that's your scene. For most locals, Mardi Gras is an all-city love fest where folks run (and bike) around in amazing, hyper-creative costumes, with the simple objective of finding and hugging your also costumed, drunken friends.

The only definitive statements that can really be made about Carnival are: don't go without a costume (ideally, Mardi Gras is all participants, no observers), and bring a little flask in your pocket (much cheaper, and you'll avoid any lines). Again though, a calm and shy person will (somehow) have as good a time at Mardi Gras as an effusive alcoholic. It's really up to you how you party. But here are some of our suggestions:

JT

DISCLAIMER

Mardi Gras is really a big messy soup of a party. As much as you want to plan to see particular things, schedules are apt to get messed up. But whatever you do see will be equally as good as what you thought you'd see.

Baby Dolls

Fat Tuesday

A group of women strutting through the streets in satin and lace baby-doll getups (that look more like French maid costumes with bonnets), continuing a black female tradition with deep and distant roots. Before her recent death, **Miss Antoinette K-Doe** had resurrected the dormant baby doll tradition, and thus a good place to catch them (*and* Mardi Gras Indians, and many other of Mardi Gras' best weird krewes,) is her **Mother-in-Law Lounge** *(1500 N. Claiborne; k-doe.com).*

Barkus Parade

two Sundays before Fat Tuesday; barkus.org

An afternoon parade featuring hundreds of hilariously costumed dogs. Also some cats, and maybe a goat or two. At around 10a.m. the animals begin gathering at Armstrong Park on Rampart St. before the parade begins at 2p.m., heading down St. Ann and winding through the French Quarter. The day culminates in a costume contest and a Barkus Ball (humans only, sorry!)

Bass Parade

late, late Lundi Gras night

In its tenth year, this parade of dozens of bass players and a few drummers begins outside the **R Bar**. Regular participants include **Dr. Jimbo Walsh, Jonathan Freilich, James Singleton, Galactic's Stanton Moore,** playing everything from Led Zep to Rick James. Check YouTube for a nice little documentary.

Bacchus

Sunday before Fat Tuesday, Uptown around Toledano and St. Charles; kreweofbacchus.org

Since 1969, the mainstream but wild Krewe of Bacchus rolls, with many small alternative krewes in tow, including the ever-entertaining **Box of Wine** krewe, who directly celebrate the Roman god of wine.

Krewe De Poux

Bywater, Lundi Gras night

A satire of the satirical parade described above, put on by bike-punks, fauxbeauxs and other colorful snowbirds and Bywater/Marigny cretins. After the parade and coronation (last year the king and queen were our cover-boy **Ratty Scurvics** and his wife **Ooops the Clown**), the krewe meets in an alley near Franklin St. in Marigny for its annual demolition derby of creatively-altered shopping carts. The carts crash and bash until only the champion is left standing – that is, if the cops don't come and break it up first. Check the YouTube documentary.

Krewe De Vieux

....

*early evening on Twelfth Night,
Mardi Gras' kickoff; kreweduvieux.
org*

For many locals, this low
budget parade of sex jokes three
weekends before Fat Tuesday
is the real kick-off of Mardi
Gras season which, technically,
began a few weeks back. Krewe
De Vieux (as in Vieux Carre,
the French name for French
Quarter) is a satirical, raunchy
parade in 19th-century Carnival
style, complete with small floats
drawn by krewe members and
mules.

The Krewe of Joyful Noise, featuring the Noisician Coalition

....

*Bacchus Sunday, Lundi Gras
midnight, but also VooDoo Fest
during Halloween, and select New
Orleans Bingo! Show gigs; myspace.
com/noisician*

With an array of self-styled
instruments, including
tubas made from drainpipes,
saxophones melded with
bullhorns and guitar-pedal-
accordion contraptions, this
ragtag krewe dressed in red and
black outfits split the sartorial
difference between steampunk,
pirate, and scary clown. Began
as an expression of **New
Orleans Bingo! Show** member
Mattvaughn Black's love of
strange noises, the Noisicians
hold several parades and a ball
throughout the year. Their main
events, however, are a trip down

the St. Charles Avenue parade
route, confusing spectators
waiting for the **Bacchus** (as
part of the lewd **Box of Wine
Krewe** parade) and a midnight
march on Lundi Gras night,
assuring them billing as the first
parade of Mardi Gras Day.

Krewe of Kosmic Debris

....

*begins at noon on Frenchmen St.,
Mardi Gras day*

Formed in 1977, this now 200-
plus person French Quarter
pub crawl parade on Mardi
Gras morn invites all comers in
costume to join in and jam on
Dixieland standards – whether
or not you know how to play an
instrument.

Muses

....

*usually on the Friday night before
Mardi Gras; kreweofmuses.org*

While the rest of the big
float parades can get a bit
monotonous, this all-female
Mardi Gras krewe has the
absolute best throws, plus the
most dynamic array of floats
and live bands. The best parade
of all Mardi Gras, hands down.

Ninth Ward Marching Band

....

*lots of places; check website for
schedule, quintronandmisspussycat.
com/marchingband*

Founded by one-man-band **Mr.
Quintron**, the 9th Ward
Marching Band began in the late
90's as a project for Bywater's

many bohemian musician types. Inspired by the musicianship, choreography and showmanship of the high school marching bands, Q and crew put together a team of thirty-odd artists and oddballs in clean, pressed red-and-white uniforms emblazoned with sparkly 9's. Because the 9th Ward is largely considered a black neighborhood, many locals roll their eyes at the nearly all-Caucasian band. Still, they've got a fun dance team, cheerleaders, a gun squad, flag girls – the whole (ahem) nine yards. The underground team has recently been welcomed by the mainstream and can now be seen in several big "official" Mardi Gras parades each year, including **Muses** and **Bacchus**.

Northside Skull and Bones Gang

early morning, Fat Tuesday, Treme

Dressed in black with papier mâché skull masks and other spooky attire, this long-standing black krewe (established in the early 19th century) delivers an early morning wake-up call to the Tremé neighborhood and "brings the spirits to the streets on Mardi Gras morning," says **Bruce "Sunpie" Barnes**, the gang's second chief.

Secret Society of St. Ann

Mardi Gras morning, some house on Clouet St. in Bywater; kreweofstanne.org

The now not-as-secret Society of St. Ann amasses early Mardi

Quintron's Ninth Ward Marching Band rolls with its 2005 Grand Marshall, pornographic girl rapper Peaches.

Gras morning on Clouet St. in the Bywater and marches into the French Quarter (to Canal Street for the big boring **Rex** parade, before doubling back to the Quarter) in some of the best most elaborate costumes Carnival has to offer.

Zulu

....

Fat Tuesday afternoon, Canal St., down St. Charles; kreweofzulu.com

This all-black krewe, dating back to the early 1900's, is active all year, and based out of the Zulu Social Aid and Pleasure Club (*732 North Broad St.*). Their parade essentially consists of black people wearing black face, making fun of the white idea that blacks are "savages." Wearing grass skirts, lard can hats, and banana stalk scepters; the krewe throws out much-coveted hand-painted Zulu coconuts. Zulu's history and calendar of yearly events are extremely dense and fascinating, and should be checked out on their website.

N.O. MOMENT:
BANJO PLAYER & LOCAL, GEOFF DOUVILLE OF EGG YOLK JUBILEE'S MARDI GRAS ADVICE

Wanna know what Mardi Gras is like for your average New Orleans musician? Just before Mardi Gras 2008, we randomly ran into Geoff Douville, a local filmmaker, guitarist, educator and banjo player in much-loved genre-defying brass-ish band Egg Yolk Jubilee. Geoff is a shining example of a local artist and neighbor.

PAUL GRASS

Geoff was sitting outside of Café Rose Nicaud on Frenchmen St. catching his breath (which admittedly smelled of a couple drinks), sweating in formal wear like he'd just come from a job (because he had just come from a job), with his shiny banjo case at his feet. "I was playing at this crazy wedding with the marching band version of Egg Yolk Jubilee," he explained. "We play another party tonight, and had some time to kill in between, so we all took our instruments and decided let's go to The Alpine off Jackson Square for a Bloody Mary. While we're in there the owner says 'Hey play for us, I'll buy a round, play a couple tunes!' So we end up drinking a few more." Geoff sighed and sipped. "Now the owner wants to hire us."

Normally, this wouldn't seem strange at all. And it definitely doesn't during Mardi Gras. Still we busted out our tape recorder and let Geoff give us some factoids about New Orleans, and his Mardi Gras suggestions, for you (drop a tip in Geoff's bucket!)

Doubloons

"As far as the stuff they throw off of floats, people only more recently switched over to wanting beads. Beads used to be small, but the demand for bare breasts drove up the size of beads. Then 10 or 15 years ago people were crazy about cups, whereas people don't even pay attention now when cups are thrown. I am on a one-man crusade to bring the doubloons back: the gold coins. Doubloons used to be the big thing when I was little. I have even been given the black doubloon: it's covered in black enamel, very treasured, the rarest, carried only by the black hooded marshal KKK-looking creepy guy on the horse that leads the parades. If you get that, you've been anointed. It means you've been chosen.

The Full Grown Man Society and Harem

myspace.com/fullgrownmansociety

"This is our parade krewe, dedicated to the promotion and preservation of the Full Grown Man Lifestyle. It's all people from New Orleans marching, people who I grew with up in the city, or that I've just known for a long, long time. The name comes from that famous blues song, "I'm A Full Grown Man." One way we express our full-grown manhood is that our parade route runs against the grain; we go down one-way streets the wrong way. We host an event called 'Chicks with Hula Hoops.' Musicians versed in traditional New Orleans Carnival Music are encouraged to participate. I'm the king next year.

High School Marching Bands

"I am a connoisseur of New Orleans high school marching bands. They are the heart and soul of any parade, and of New Orleans itself. And their sound is honed by the frequency of Mardi Gras, and the fact that band directors have been participating in Mardi Gras for years and years. A lot of high school marching bands are only now getting it back together since Katrina. I really support that **Roots of Music Foundation** *(www.therootsofmusic.com)* started by **Derrick Tabb** of **ReBirth Brass Band,** that busses kids out to learn marching band music when middle school programs are cut.

Parades

"I always go to **Endymion in Mid-City**, and the all-female **Muses** parade. I usually go to the **The Krewe of MidCity,** which has been moved to Uptown; they have unique floats made of tinfoil, tinfoil decorations, it's totally unique, plus they are *the* marching band parade. I always love playing in **Krewe De Vieux** with the **9th Ward Marching Band.** And this year I played in something called the **T-Rex parade**, which I agreed to knowing only that I had to dress up like a giant. Turned out all the floats were miniature, shoebox sized, and they rolled them down the street like regular floats.

Lee Circle

"Watch the parades under the **Calliope** overpass at Lee Circle. There is this reverb under that bridge, and the high school marching bands always play at that moment. They do their best routine, to hear it in that monstrous reverb. Plus since it's a circle, you get the chance to see the bands twice.

Real banjos

"I play banjo, but not like the fauxbeauxs. I play a real four-string New Orleans tenor banjo, just like my great uncle who played with **Louis Prima**, who is also from New Orleans. New Orleans banjo playing is specific to here, it evolved out of here. The funkballs try to imitate it, but their banjos are the five string Appalachian, for country bluegrass, which has an extra "drone string." The four-string New Orleans banjo don't have that extra string and aren't meant to be finger-plucked but strummed, like jazz chords."

FESTIVALS AND HOLIDAYS

JT

A slightly buzzed tourist eats a turkey leg and frustratedly scans the festival scene for somewhere to sit.

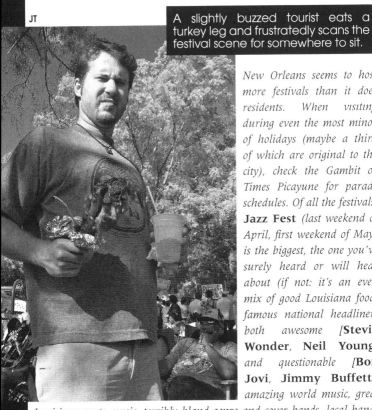

New Orleans seems to host more festivals than it does residents. When visiting during even the most minor of holidays (maybe a third of which are original to the city), check the Gambit or Times Picayune for parade schedules. Of all the festivals, **Jazz Fest** (last weekend of April, first weekend of May) is the biggest, the one you've surely heard or will hear about (if not: it's an even mix of good Louisiana food, famous national headliners both awesome [**Stevie Wonder**, **Neil Young**] and questionable [**Bon Jovi**, **Jimmy Buffett**,] amazing world music, great Louisiana roots music, terribly bland genre and cover bands, local bands locals've seen a million times under better conditions for cheaper but that you'll nonetheless flip over, plus hellish heat, frustrating crowds) so we won't harp on jazz fest. Here are some other popular, lesser known, and fringe New Orleans fests (for more info, check out **Louisiana Music Factory**'s festivals guide at Louisiana-festivals.com)

Alternative Media Expo
....
March-ish; myspace.com/ alternativemediaexpo

Another project by **AntiGravity** music magazine publisher **Leo McGovern**, who's known for turning small, simple grassroots ideas into real winners. His Alt Media Expo – usually held at the

Contemporary Arts Center (CAC) just after Mardi Gras (March-ish) – features anything and everything wordy and visual. A stunning presentation of dozens of New Orleans and national comix publishers, literary concerns, makers of indie movies and websites and statement clothing, etc. And of course in true New Orleans fashion, the Expo also features good food and booze, and both the pre *and* post Expo parties always feature bands.

Bayou Boogaloo

May, Mid-City, at Bayou St. John; thebayouboogaloo.com

This laid-back, family-friendly fest is fairly new; it was organized as a morale-booster for the flooded Mid-City neighborhood, which has been recovering by leaps and bounds. The Boogaloo takes place on the banks of Bayou St. John, for two days on three stages, with a mix of marquee-name and neighborhood-favorite zydeco, funk, rock and Latin music. In 2009, the festival went 100% green, with solar-powered stages, biodiesel generators and organic snacks.

Blues and BBQ Festival

Mid-October, CBD, Lafayette Square Park, 600 S. Maestri Pl., 504.558.6100; jazzandheritage.org/blues-fest

Free, two-day festival of big name blues artists and food.

Cajun Zydeco Festival

Mid June, French Quarter, French Market, 1008 N. Peters St., 504.558.6100; jazzandheritage.org/cajun-zydeco

Free, two-day festival of traditional zydeco music on two stages, down by the river in the **French Market**. Given its location, it feels a bit touristy, but the music is the real deal.

FESTIVALS

Washboard Chaz entertains the crowd at ChazFest.

Chazfest

....

Wednesday between the two weekends of Jazz Fest, Bywater, Truck Farm Studios, 3024 Saint Claude Ave, 504-944-7776; chazfestival.com

Conceived as a balm for the egos of a group of downtown musicians who weren't booked at Jazz Fest one year, Chazfest is the Bywater's companion piece to the monster fest. Named in honor of the prolific, quirky bluesman **Washboard Chaz**, Chazfest is organized by Chaz's sideman, singer and guitarist **Alex McMurray**. Held in the communal yard of the **Truck Farm** (a recording studio owned by **Dave Pirner** of **Soul Asylum**), this fest features excellent downtown groups like the **Happy Talk Band**, brass bands, side projects like McMurray's sea-shanty outfit the **Valparaiso Men's Chorus** and of course, Chaz. Admission is usually $25 (about a third the cost of actual Jazz Fest). You still have to pay for (cheaper) drinks and (great) food. But for those adverse to huge crowds, and who want to socialize and drink with some of the city's best musicians rather than stare at them from afar, Chazfest may indeed be a better alternative.

Concert in the Park Series

....

Thursday afternoons in Spring, CBD, Lafayette Square Park, 500 St. Charles Ave., 504-881-9861; lafayettesquare.org

The free *Concert in the Park* series caters to more touristy notions of New Orleans music (you will likely hear "When the Saints Go Marching In"), even though most concert attendees are locals just getting off work. Since you're just visiting however, it's worth spreading a blanket in the shade and chillin' in the park for a couple hours.

Congo Square Rhythms Festival

....

Mid-November, Treme, Louis Armstrong Park, 901 N. Rampart St., 504.558.6100; jazzandheritage. org/congo-square

A celebration of the point at which Africa and New Orleans intersect. Along with jazz and African drumming, this fest always features rappers and a parade.

Creole Tomato Festival

....

June, French Quarter, French Market, 1008 N. Peters St., 504.558.6100

Food booths offer Creole Tomato favorites like Fried Green Tomatoes, Creole Tomato Bloody Marys, Stuffed Shrimp with Grilled Creole, Creole Tomato Cream Crawfish Pies, Blooming Onion on a bed of Creole Tomato and more. Plus cooking demonstrations, music and dancing throughout the weekend.

Essence Festival

Forth of July weekend, CBD,
Louisiana Superdome, Sugar
Bowl Dr. 1-800-756-7074;
essencemusicfestival.com

Though many in New Orleans wish mayor Ray Nagin hadn't called New Orleans a "chocolate city" so soon after Katrina, it wasn't like the dude was lying. Almost everything truly great about the city has come from its majority black population – New Orleans is indeed the choclatiest of cities. So it makes sense that **Essence Magazine** would hold its annual festival of mainstream Black music, authors, and empowerment seminars here. The food and drinks are expensive and not so special (inside, that is; the unlicensed vendors outside the Superdome can blow your mind, cheaply), and Essence Fest's consumer-oriented focus can be vaguely nauseating (corporate logos anywhere they can fit 'em). But much of the music is amazing: from **Al Green** to **Beyonce,** to the city's best brass bands like **The Soul Rebels**. As are the attendees' hairdos and other wildly elegant fashion statements; "dress to impress" is the hard and fast rule at Essence Fest, where indoors sunglasses are *de rigueur*.

French Quarter Fest

Early to mid April, along
the Mississippi; fqfi.org/
frenchquarterfest

Still considered by some locals to be an "alternative" to the big festival, there's barely room to walk along the river and lines for food and drinks can get huge at French Quarter Fest. FQF lacks the cheesy national headliners of Jazz Fest, and is certainly more local (and free!) still the musicians often overdo the 'entertain the tourists' shtick since they're playing in the Quarter. Still, you will find some less self-conscious music here if you're in the right place at the right time.

Harvest Music Series

Thursday afternoons in Fall,
CBD, Lafayette Square Park, 500
St. Charles Ave., 504-881-9861;
lafayettesquare.org

Same as the *Concert in the Park* series detailed above, except proceeds benefit the **Second Harvest Food Bank of Greater New Orleans and Acadiana**.

Mid-Summer Mardi Gras

End of hot-ass August, begins at
Maple Leaf Bar, 8316 Oak St.,
Uptown

We maybe should clarify that sometimes when we say "parades," we mean events which lack observers – only participants. For more than 20 years, the **Krewe of O.A.K.** (acronym for "outrageous and kinky," they claim, but the parade also starts on Oak St.) has celebrated a faux Mardi Gras with this glorified pub-crawl, six months after the actual Fat Tuesday. Floats in this "parade" are generally decorated golf

FESTIVALS

carts, rolling between brass bands and a sweating, drunk, dancing crowd. The heat keeps the mandatory costumes skin-oriented.

Mirliton Festival
....
November, Bywater, Markey Park, corner of Royal and Piety streets; mirlitonfestival.com

great mix of traditional and fringe neighborhood bands. Mirliton Fest is a big deal to hundreds of neighbors and musicians, and yet always feels wonderfully mellow.

New Orleans Film Festival
....
Mid-October, 504-309-6633; neworleansfilmfest.com

Keith "Deacon Johnson" Moore, now deceased son of famous New Orleans R&B artist Deacon John, and founder of NOize Fest.

ZS

This important, well-attended Bywater neighborhood festival pays homage to a seasonal squash-like vegetable with little taste and little function. In **Markey Park**, most of the Bywater/Marigny's restaurants rise to the challenge of making something delectable out of the mirliton. The beer is cheap, and the fest is usually a

The New Orleans Film Society presents this truly excellent, seven-day jam-packed festival of regional and national independent feature films, shorts, documentaries, animation works, and experimental pieces. There are also dozens of panels and workshops (Finding Funding, Women in Film,

Film Sound), directors' meet-and-greet receptions, and after-parties featuring high profile music like **Dr. John**. Most of the action takes place at Canal Street Cinema (*French Quarter, 333 Canal St # 327, 504-581-5400; landmarktheatres.com*) and Prytania Theatre (*Uptown, 5339 Prytania St., 504-891-2787; theprytania.com*), but keep an eye on their website for exact details and schedules.

NOizeFest
....
First Sunday of May, last day of Jazz Fest, Bywater, 609 Lesseps St.; myspace.com/noizefestnola

NOizeFest's inventor **Keith "Deacon Johnson" Moore** was the son of **Deacon John**, the famous R&B singer who played guitar on almost every famous New Orleans record ever. Keith came up with NOizeFest out of anger at JazzFest for ignoring all the non-traditional/experimental/original music that is nonetheless part of the lifeblood of the city. After Keith was shot and killed uptown in 2005, his friends continued the fest in Michael Patrick Welch's backyard. which was big enough to accommodate simultaneous multiple performers, but comfy enough to allow for serious sonic overlap. NOizeFest's anti "band" lineup runs the gamut from DJs to tape manipulators, to an all-noise marching band, to well-know acts like **Mr. Quintron**, doing everything but his usual dance-rock. Recently some classical musicians have braved the fest's noisy waters, taking it

to a new level. But in true New Orleans fashion, all 12 hours of the fest are usually giddy, unpretentious fun.

Po-Boy Preservation Festival
....
End of November, Uptown, Oak St.; poboyfest.com

A seven-block party in celebration of the mammoth sandwich of French bread and fried seafood or roast beef. Of course you'll find many more dynamic variations on the cultural staple at this fest, which also hosts two stages of music, over 60 artists, a children's section with games, a po-boy photo booth, and panel discussions covering the po-boy's history.

Ponderosa Stomp
....
Mid September, French Quarter, 225 Decatur St.; ponderosastomp.com

Started in 2007 as the wedding reception for a local anesthesiologist with a massive vinyl collection, the P-Stomp has grown into an internationally renowned record geek's wet dream. It draws fans that often completely ignore JazzFest in favor of a midweek smorgasbord of obscure R&B, soul, garage, rockabilly and country from the South and beyond. Psychedelic madman **Roky Erickson** is a regular performer, as are **Stax** and **Hi Soul Men William Bell** and **Teenie Hodges**. Recently, the Stomp has added

FESTIVALS

daytime conference sessions at the Louisiana State Museum to the slate of offerings, with live interviews conducted by historians like **Peter Gurlanick** and crate-digger royalty like Norton Records' **Billy Miller** and **Miriam Linna.** The fest began in the amazing **Rock-n-Bowl** bowling alley and concert hall, but unfortunately switched in the last couple years to a corporate venue. The music though, remains as good as ever.

Satchmo Summer Fest

....

four days at the end of July/ beginning of August, Marigny/ French Quarter; fqfi.org/ satchmosummerfest

A family-oriented, fat weekend of jazz music and food celebrating the life of **Louis Armstrong**. Again, the music is very traditional, but New Orleans mellows out dramatically this late in the summer, making Satchmo less crowded and less expensive than the other fests.

N.O. MOMENT:

IRA "DR. IKE" PADNOS
CREATOR OF THE
PONDEROSA STOMP

"Dr. Ike" Padnos is the ringleader of the cabal of rabid music fans behind the **Ponderosa Stomp**, a record-geek mecca of a music festival held in New Orleans since 2002. Ira, an actual doctor (anesthesiologist) originally from Chicago, was already a freakishly knowledgeable record collector when he attended Tulane in the '80s; now he's got most of the legendary and obscure musicians who shaped American rock n'roll in his cell phone.

How did the Stomp start?

Basically, I used to throw once-a-year parties in the backyard, and it was getting bigger and bigger. When I got married, I wanted to do something special, so I went through my record collection and tried to get as many people that I'd always wanted to see to come play my wedding. It ran the gamut from **Hubert Sumlin** to **Paul Burleson** to **Billy Lee Riley** to **James Burton** to **Jody Williams** to **Classie Ballou**. It went on all night, and then one of my wedding guests told me we had to bring these people to the public in New Orleans.

When you were going to school here, what was your definitive New Orleans musical experience?

One thing that will always stick in my mind is going to see **The Meters** at **Tipitina's** for the first time in 1983. Or seeing **Earl King** at Mardi Gras totally drunk and fried from being out all day; Earl's band changed out three times during the course of the set. Or the **Mardi Gras Indians**. But basically just the whole city – it's somewhere else, there's nowhere else like it. Going home for summer breaks was like another world.

If you had some musical advice for a tourist who was coming to New Orleans and reading this guidebook, what would it be?

One thing is that a guidebook is good for some stuff, but you have to try to find stuff, dig deeper, listen to **WWOZ** or **WTUL**. They'll always point you in the right direction for something that's a little bit different. **The Saturn Bar** is definitely a place that people should go. It's pretty wild. It's a fun place. **The Mother-in-Law** is another great place.

What about food? Where should visitors eat?

One place you'll never find in a guidebook is the all-time killer place where chickens go to die: **Mr. Roosevelt's Black Pearl** (*1001 N. Claiborne Ave. corner of St. Philip , 504-827-5770*). It has awesome soul food and on Friday afternoons, stuffed bell peppers and stuffed crabs that are incredible. All-time favorite place.

Southern Decadence

....

Labor Day weekend, French Quarter, Bourbon St.; southerndecadence.net

For many, many years this gay sex party was extreme enough to make Mardi Gras blush – everything, just everything, going on right out there on Bourbon Street! Until some religious group pointed out to the city that public sex was against the law, and made the taxpayers spend hundreds of thousands on security for an event at which no one had ever been arrested. Decadence still goes off every year, but is now much mellower. Sunday is still alive with ultra-flamboyant cross-dressers and leather studs, all culminating in an excellent drag parade that's totally fun for everyone. And one must assume that *something* kinky is still cooking behind all those tall French Quarter gates.

St. Patrick's Day

....

March 15, Uptown; irishchannelno.org

The Irish Channel St. Patrick's Day Club holds its annual Mass and drinking celebration every March 15, beginning at noon at St. Mary's Assumption Church (corner of Constance and Josephine streets), followed by a huge parade with generous throws, that starts at the corner of Felicity and Magazine at 1p.m. Parade goers are pelted with traditional Irish vegetables (cabbages, potatoes, carrots etc.) by hundreds of Irish men and women in formal attire either riding atop Mardi Gras-sized floats, or walking in drunken groups, collecting kisses in exchange for flowers.

Thanksgiving at Fair Grounds Race Course & Slots

....

1751 Gentilly Blvd., 504-944-5515; fairgroundsracecourse.com

On many special occasions throughout the year in New Orleans, Black people dress to the nines and go out in public. The older Black gentlemen especially, will kick your ass in the style department. But the one time of the year where white folks also get gussied up for the express purpose of showing off, is the opening day of horse racing at New Orleans' Fair Grounds (the site of our annual **Jazz & Heritage Fest**). The food is amazing, the drinks are strong, everything's pretty cheap (entry is free!) and every sector of New Orleans humanity is represented – and thus, friendship and holiday love hang thick in the air. But again, dress mad stylish, and don't forget a bad-ass hat of some sort.

The Tennessee Williams New Orleans Literary Festival

....

end of March, French Quarter; tennesseewilliams.net

This is the big old festival of famous, talented, and topical writers of fiction, plays, even screenplays, all with a concentration on (but not a bias for) the regional, and on anyone who's written any book or made any documentary about famous Southern playwright Tennessee Williams. This fest is also chock full of writing business workshops and agents, for aspiring writers looking to plan a working vacation to New Orleans. The fest's most memorable act however, is usually its "Stella!" contest, wherein contests compete to hear who's best at yelling that phrase up at a balcony, replicating the famous scene from Williams' *A Streetcar Named Desire*.

Voodoo Music Experience

End of October, Halloween weekend, Mid-City, City Park, corner of Esplanade and Carrollton; thevoodooexperience.com

New Orleans' only festival of nationally famous alternative rock bands, The Voodoo Music Experience in City Park makes Halloween weekend in New Orleans just that much more of an event. From **TV on the Radio** to **Nine Inch Nails** to **R.E.M.** to **Kiss**, to the **Bingo!** tent, which features the upper echelon of truly original New Orleans musicians. There's even a small **Preservation Hall** tent if you just *have to* hear "the standards." Voodoo's best quality though may be its location in City Park; whereas JazzFest puts you in direct contact with the sun for long hours with barely any shelter, much of City Park is shaded by giant oak trees, which also serve to break up the VooDoo crowd and dilute that claustrophobic festival feeling.

The White Bitch in the Bingo! tent at VooDoo Fest 2009

MORGANA KING

N.O. MOMENT

NEW ORLEANS FILM FESTIVAL

EACH OCTOBER

NEWORLEANSFILMSOCIETY.ORG

Even before the film industry exploded in this state, the **New Orleans Film Festival** was an impressive, week-long event filled with screenings, parties and panels. Celebrating its 22nd anniversary this October, the festival showcased more local films than ever.

Although the festival does not specifically seek out local film submissions, there is so much grassroots film activity here, many New Orleans-made features, documentaries, and shorts are getting into this highly selective festival. The festival has even added an "I Love Louisiana Day" to celebrate this trend.

In addition to featuring some great, local shorts like **Ashley Charbonnet's** *The Price of Flowers*, this year's "I Love Louisiana Day" also premiered the homegrown, narrative feature, **Flood Streets** (www.floodstreetsmovie. com). Lovingly shot on a shoestring budget, this character-driven pic follows a group of creative malcontents as they struggle to find love, money and marijuana in the surreal streets of post-flood New Orleans. Written by long-time Bywater resident **Helen**

Krieger and directed by her husband **Joseph Meissner**, who also plays one of the leads, Flood Streets shows off the new sounds of New Orleans music, bands like the **Zydepunks**, **Panorama Jazz Band**, **Debauche**, and **Meschiya Lake**. It also features New Orleans-adapted comedian Harry Shearer in two very funny cameos. A nuanced look at the city after the storm, this film has been winning awards at festivals across the country. They have more screenings coming up and a soundtrack album due out soon, so keep abreast of it all at.

The New Orleans Film Society (neworleansfilmsociety. org) that organizes the festival schedules other film-related events throughout the year like panels, special screenings, and drive-up "theaters" at abandoned parking lots across town. What better use for a flooded strip mall?

M WELSH

Singer Meschiya Lake in the second-line scene from 100% local movie "Flood Streets".

LITERARY NEW ORLEANS

From **Tennessee Williams** *to* **William S. Burroughs** *(whose house on the Westbank (509 Wagner St.), where* **Kerouac** *visited him in* On the Road, *is inscribed with a plaque), from* **William Faulkner** *to* **Truman Capote** *to* **Charles Bukowski** *(whose first two books were published from an apartment on Royal St.),* **Anne Rice**, **Walker Percy**, **Andrei Codrescu** *(who in our sidebar suggests all serious writers visit* **The Goldmine Saloon** *(French Quarter, 703 Dauphine St. for Thursday night readings), and poor old* **John Kennedy Toole** *(whose novel* A Confederacy of Dunces *won a Pulitzer shortly after Toole killed himself, partly because he couldn't find a publisher), New Orleans has always been a writer's paradise: cheap, wild, inspiring, boozy – with tons of bookstores:*

LITERARY EVENTS

Alternative Media Expo

March-ish; myspace.com/ alternativemediaexpo

Independently published books are just one part of this festival put on by **AntiGravity** music magazine publisher **Leo McGovern**. Usually held at the **Contemporary Arts Center (CAC)** just after Mardi Gras (March-ish), the AME features dozens of New Orleans and national comix publishers, literary concerns, makers of indie movies and websites and statement clothing, etc.

in independent publishing, anarchist literature, zine culture, plus all types of singular, handmade pieces of art that happen to be books. Most good cities have a bookfair, but New Orleans' becomes a bit of a party, that can even get a little wild – the official annual after-party was held one year in an abandoned YMCA. As the DJ spun great rap, everyone danced and played basketball, got wasted and rode their bikes around the gym crazily. Somehow the cops never came. And everyone walked away with a *lot* of good books.

New Orleans Book Fair

around Halloween; nolabookfair.com

One more reason to visit New Orleans as October turns into November is our giant **New Orleans Book Fair,** featuring all the biggest names

Saints and Sinners

mid-May; sasfest.org

This Marigny literary festival features the top names in the gay and lesbian publishing/literary world. Saints and Sinners is curated in part by **Otis Fennell**, owner of **Faubourg Marigny**

Art and Books *(see Frenchmen Street in Music Clubs section)*, who also manages the literary angle of New Orleans' **Pride Festival** *(June; www.gayprideneworleans. com)* in Washington Square Park on Frenchmen St.

The Tennessee Williams New Orleans Literary Festival

....

end of March, tennesseewilliams.net

This is the big old festival of famous, talented, and topical writers of fiction, plays, even screenplays, all with a concentration on (but not a bias for) the regional, and on anyone who's written any book or made any documentary about famous Southern playwright Tennessee Williams. This fest is also chock full of writing business workshops and agents, for aspiring writers looking to plan a working vacation to New Orleans. The fest's most memorable act however, is usually its "Stella!" contest, wherein contests compete to hear who's best at yelling that phrase up at balcony, replicating the famous scene from Williams' *A Streetcar Named Desire.*

N.O. MOMENT:

NEIGHBORHOOD STORY PROJECT: THE BEST NEW ORLEANS SOUVENIRS YOU COULD POSSIBLY BUY

ARTS

RACHEL BREUNLIN

Abram Himelstein and **Rachel Breunlin** are two young teachers who believe that New Orleans' story must be told by the people who live it. With that in mind, Abram and Rachel began **The Neighborhood Story Project**, which in 2008 opened its own office and writing workshop area in the 7th Ward (*corner of Miro and Lapeyrouse streets*). Anyone is welcome to pop in, tour the office, get free writing advice and guidance and maybe even a book advance if you're local. As of this writing, since 2004 the NSP has published eight well-received books, all borne from the brains of regular New Orleanians – both adults and children – most documenting the nuanced struggles and celebrations of various neighborhoods, **Mardi Gras Indian** tribes, Social Aid and Pleasure clubs, and other New Orleans phenomena of which the outer world knows little.

RACHEL BREUNLIN

ARTS

The NSP's books are among the best independent, grassroots sellers in the city. *Coming Out the Door For the Ninth Ward*, written by and about the members of the **Nine Times Social Aid & Pleasure Club**, has sold close to 5,000 books and has yet to be put through a distributor. The organization's most recent book (as of this writing) is a 200-page, full-color tome called *The House of Dance and Feathers, a Museum* by Ronald Lewis, based on the museum Lewis built in his back yard in the Lower 9th Ward, on Tupelo Street (also see Art Galleries). House of Dance and Feathers details the world of Mardi Gras Indians: how it works, who sews patches, what those relationships are like. Ronald then takes readers through the Social Aid and Pleasure Club world and that of the **Northside Skull and Bones Gang**, and in the process maps the history of the Lower 9th Ward.

If you can't make it down to the NSP's offices, all their books are sold at most New Orleans bookstores. You couldn't possibly buy a better souvenir of your trip to the city..

N.O. MOMENT:

Author CHARLES BUKOWSKI
FIT RIGHT IN HERE

If not for New Orleans, Charles Bukowski may have amounted to nothing. This city played just as big a part in his career as it did **Faulkner's**. In the documentary *The Outsiders of New Orleans: Loujon Press*, **Louise "Gypsy Lou" Webb** – now well into her nineties and currently living in the burbs of Slidell – tells how she and her husband **Jon Webb** published the avant-garde literary magazine *The Outsider* from a small apartment on the corner of **Royal St**. and **Ursuline Ave**. in the French Quarter in the early 1960's. *The Outsider* and Bukowski's first two books by **Loujon Press** (*loujonpress.com*) – *It Catches My Heart In It's Hands* and *Crucifix in a Deathhand* – are now rare collectibles, along with two other handcrafted books by **Henry Miller**. Bukowski cavorted around the Quarter drinking and fighting with strangers while the Webbs labored over his

work in their apartment. At some point he etched "Hank was here" in the cement outside of the **R Bar** (*1431 Royal St.*). For the longest time, one of the guest rooms the author had rented upstairs from R Bar was called "The Bukowski Suite." Somehow that wasn't a big selling point, and the name was recently changed.

GRAZIANO ORIGA (2008 CREATIVE COMMONS)

BOOKSTORES

Beckham's

French Quarter, 228 Decatur St.,
504-522-9875

Beckham's looks like a used bookstore in a movie about New Orleans, with a rolling ladder to access upper shelves, where you might find a book of spells – though you're more likely to find classic literature. Near the front door is always a good selection of new local novels, cookbooks and whatnot, and the upstairs is loaded with classical music LPs for sale, and more books. Truly a gorgeous place. (*see* COFFEESHOPS)

Beth's Books

Marigny, 2700 Chartres St.,
504-947-4477

Beth's Books shares a building with Sound Café and specializes in high-quality used books, plus tons of titles by New Orleans authors.

Crescent City Comics

Uptown, 4916 Freret St.;
504-891-3796

Crescent City Comics re-opened at an Uptown location in the fall of 2009 after being knocked out of business by Katrina. Whether you're well-read in comics or trying one for the first time, you'll find a vast selection of independent and underground comics and graphic novels, your favorite superheroes, and a friendly staff. The shop also doubles as the office for the local music magazine, **AntiGravity**.

Iron Rail Book Collective

French Quarter; 503 Barracks St.
504-383-3284; ironrail.org

Collective-run, non-profit, anarchist book store, record store, and lending library. Too small for shows, but a possible space for organizational meetings or reading/speaking engagements.

Maple St. Books

Uptown, 7523 Maple St.,
New Orleans, 504-866-4916;
maplestreetbookshop.com

One of New Orleans' most famous, and tiniest, bastions of liberal thought for over 30 years. Serious **Walker Percy** fans take note: Maple Leaf had an ongoing relationship with the author, who did many readings there until his death.

Garden District Books

Uptown; 2727 Prytania Street
New Orleans, LA 70130-5968
(504) 895-2266

Garden District is in a building converted from a 19th centruy skating rink. The staff actually read the books they sell, which can't be said of the nearby chain bookstore.

N.O. MOMENT:

FAUBOURG MARIGNY ART AND BOOKS (F.A.B.)
OWNER, OTIS FENNELL

ZS

The gay and straight bookstore **Faubourg Marigny Art and Books** (see *Bookstores* in the *Literary* section) first opened in 1977. When in 2003 the original owner decided to call it a day, Otis Fennell bought the store, simply to save a cultural institution. "Now that **Oscar Wilde**'s in Greenwich Village has closed," Otis says, "FAB might be the only bookstore of its type in the states. You'll go all over the country and not find anything like this."

Though thoroughly gay-seeming from the outside, FAB carries one of the city's best selections of both straight and gay New Orleans-bred literature, alongside a nice selection of new national releases and worn classics. Otis also hosts readings by nationally famous, mostly gay authors, almost weekly. But regardless of sexual orientation, you'll want to stop in and talk to Otis, who has lived in and (actively participated in) New Orleans for 50 years. Especially since buying FAB, Otis has become the don of Frenchmen, standing beside the rainbow Napoleon statue outside of his shop on the corner of Chartres every single day from noon to midnight. "I'm open late because the street is a late-night spot," he smiles, watching the crowds pass.

Otis has also changed the store by adding much more local art; under his reign, FAB has become essentially the only de facto art gallery on Frenchmen. "I also represent Frenchmen's musicians by selling their music in my store," says Otis. "Mainly the classic CDs and albums. I have a 30-year-old **Dr. John** LP, but I also have new bands like **Why Are We Building Such a Big Ship?** (see *Musicians*) – who, incidentally, got their start on the corner across the street. That corner continues to attract music all day and night."

FAB becomes more and more important as Frenchmen becomes more like the French Quarter; if Otis were to for some reason give up, Starbucks would surely pay stacks for such prime real estate. But for now, "FAB is the cultural anchor of Frenchmen Street," Otis brags. "My goal is to make the bookstore responsive to this street and the people who live in this neighborhood. So that even if people are only coming to New Orleans to drink and eat and shop and hear music, at least they're doing it in a real New Orleans neighborhood."

When asked – not only as a gay man but as a longtime New Orleans resident – to outline his idea of the perfect visit to the city, Otis replied, "I would start the day off early at **Croissant D'Or** (*617 Ursulines Avenue*) coffee shop on Ursulines in the quarter, the most authentic French coffee shop in the country – then head *immediately* back to Frenchmen Street! Stopping along the way, of course, for some alternative furniture shopping on lower Decatur Street, which has amazing antique shops and second-hand stores. I'd stroll up and down Frenchmen, then maybe order food from **Verte Mart** (*1201 Royal St., 504-525-4767*): a major 24-hour French Quarter deli with excellent delivery – their 24-hour liquor delivery has killed more than a few people. Then I'd maybe head into the Bywater to go for a dip at **The Country Club** (*634 Louisa St. New Orleans, LA 70117*) on Louisa Street if it's the weekend; weekends are the best times to visit the oldest clothing-optional pool in the South. Then at night I would just stay on Frenchmen St. hopping from club to club hearing who knows how many live bands."

Otis also recommends visiting near Halloween for the giant **New Orleans Book Fair** (*www.nolabookfair.com*), featuring all the biggest names in independent publishing. Otis himself helps curate the **Saints and Sinners** literary festival (*www.sasfest.org*) in mid-May, featuring the top names in the gay and lesbian publishing/literary world, as well as the literary aspects of the **Pride Festival** (*www.gayprideneworleans.com*) in June, in Washington Square Park on Frenchmen St.

More Fun Comics

Uptown, 8200 Oak St., 504-865-1800; myspace.com/mfcnola

The first comic shop open on the entire Gulf Coast, run by **D.C. Harbold** who leads the musical ventures **Dr. A-Go-Go** and **Clockwork Elvis** (see *Bands*).

McKeown's Books and Difficult Music

Uptown, 4737 Tchoupitoulas St., 504-895-1954; mckeownsbooks.com

A wide selection of used books from novels to interesting math texts, plus local releases both literary and musical. McKeown's also hosts mostly acoustic concerts by New Orleans' more scholarly abstract/noise

Octavia Books

Uptown, 513 Octavia St. [corner of Laurel], 504-899-READ; octaviabooks.com

As eclectic and "local" as anything in the French Quarter, but also a tad smarter and classier than your local chain bookstore. The staff works tirelessly to keep up with local titles, and small but amazing titles from national indie presses. At great readings featuring well-known and local authors, Octavia never forgets the wine and cheese. The shop is a wee bit tricky to find in what at first seems like too residential an area, but it's so worth the effort.

musicians. Noon to 8pm daily.

> See both acoustic and electronic experimental music while buying used books at McKeowen's Books and Difficult Music.

ZS

N.O. MOMENT:

AUTHOR ANDREI CODRESCU: BRIEF EXCEPTIONS MADE FOR INCONTESTABLE BEAUTY

Andrei Codrescu is New Orleans' most revered active writer of serious literature, and perhaps the most prolific author alive on Earth: seemingly hundreds of books so far, from his first, *Blood Countess*, to his newest (as of this writing) **The Posthuman Dada Guide: Tzara and Lenin Play Chess** (*Princeton University Press*) – plus the Peabody award-winning film *Road Scholar* and probably a hundred NPR pieces. NPR surely loves Codrescu (who is originally from Romania) as much for

EDUARD KELLER

his poetic, funny and robust insights and stories, as they do the honest-to-god Transylvanian accent in which he tells them.

We emailed Codrescu hoping we could call and let him casually hold forth regarding his favorite New Orleans haunts. Instead he composed something new, for you:

ARTS

Crescent City Books

....

French Quarter, 204 Chartres St. 800.5446.4013; commonwealthbooks.com

This is the ideal bookstore and hangout for the lover of letters: two-stories of rare and well-chosen books, a cornucopia assembled by **Joe Phillips**, the publisher also of **Black Widow Press**. The glorious afternoon light of a lazy cloudy New Orleans sky pours from the Mississippi River with the occasional sounds of a steamboat calliope. Upstairs there is a couch for quiet reading, a couch where I have often seen a melancholy youth with a leather-bound notebook, copying passages from **Tzara** or **Reverdy**. Black Widow Press is the chief publisher of surrealist and avant-garde poetry in the U.S., and all their books, shelved together here, create a dense atmosphere of mystery and magic. The Crescent City bookstore is the perfect place to spend the afternoon of a free weekday.

The Gold Mine Saloon

French Quarter, 705 Dauphine St., 504-586-0745; goldminesaloon.net

The padrone, Dave Brinks, is a great poet (author of CAVEAT ONUS, the Katrina poem for my money), who has been hosting America's best non-mainstream poets every Thursday and beyond for over six years. **Lawrence Ferlinghetti**, **Alice Notley**, **Bill Berkson**, and **Lorenzo Thomas** have read here, among hundreds of others. The Gold Mine is among the foremost poetry venue in the United States today, on a par with St. Marks' Poetry Project in New York and City Lights Books in San Francisco. Like all great poetry halls, the Gold Mine is a great place to meet well-read, intelligent, sexy and adventurous people. (authors' note: Goldmine also has a huge, beautiful collection of classic video games, many from the early 80s).

Molly's at the Market

French Quarter, 1107 Decatur St., 504-525-5169; mollysatthemarket.net

A glorious 24-hour bar with a clientele that changes every hour and consists of many layers of society, from the demimonde to judges and slumming movie stars. Molly's literary claim to fame is The Window, where on weekends writers, journalists, retired teachers and proven wits, meet to comment on the passing parade. This is a relatively closed society with a merciless streak, but there are brief exceptions made for Incontestable Beauty. The back bar at Molly's, nicknamed "Cuba" features a mural of past and present luminaries. New Orleans' Algonquin, as Molly's is sometimes called, is best between the hours of two and three a.m. when show girls get off work and relax.

Envie Café

French Quarter, 1241 Decatur St., 504-524-3689

Where the literary adventurer who sampled the above three locales can have a terrific breakfast with a hair-of-the-dog Bloody Mary, and spend the morning using the Internet or writing poetry. When the revived writer lifts her half-lidded eyes from the screen, she will see a pullulating humanity of heavily tattooed half-dressed hipsters with their dogs lying at their feet, drinking strong black coffee laced with rum, reading, smoking, and discussing sedition and pleasure. Spectacular bohemians can be glimpsed here in their own milieu, unselfconscious and feral.

ART GALLERIES

New Orleans' visual art scene may have long played second fiddle, recognition-wise, to attractions like music and food – but the same playful, liberated, indulgent attitudes that created the conditions for those pleasures have also encouraged a vibrant arts community. The city's art can sometimes be too self-referential, pandering to touristy notions of "outsider art." But with a push from international art biennial Prospect 1, which called New Orleans home in 2008, the city's underground art scene has come out fighting. The tons of new high-quality funky galleries in Bywater/Marigny now call themselves **The St. Claude Arts District** *(scadnola.com), and provide a much welcome compliment to the already existing* **Julia Street** *galleries, which are nice, but maybe a lil too mainstream. Altogether though, New Orleans can now proudly brag on its art scene:*

ST. CLAUDE ARTS DISTRICT

A more casual tableaux in a gallery off St. Claude.

Antenna Gallery

....

Bywater, 3161 Burgundy St., 504-813-4848; antennagallery.org

An anchor of the St. Claude Arts District, Antenna hosts a mixed media bag of local and national artists working in everything from film to fabric. They're operated by the local **Press Street Collective**, a 501c3 group that promotes visual art as well as literature.

Barrister's Gallery

Bywater, 2331 St. Claude Ave., 504-525-2767/ 504-710-4506; barristersgallery.com

Recently moved to St. Claude Ave. from the original smaller French Quarter storefront and a short-lived sprawling Central City space, Barrister's has a permanent collection of strange folk, outsider and ethnographic art from Africa, Haiti and Asia. The gallery also brings in a monthly-featured contemporary exhibit in keeping with their focus on the eclectic, unorthodox and freaky.

The Front

Bywater, 4100 St. Claude Ave., nolafront.org

This talented collective gallery is spearheaded by **Kyle Bravo** and **Jenny LeBlanc** who also run **Hot Iron Press**, a printing company specializing in gorgeously original chapbooks. The Front is the most meticulous and "professional" seeming gallery in the St. Claude Arts District. Open noon to 5p.m. Saturday and Sunday.

Gallery 2514

Marigny, 2514 St. Claude Ave., 504-914-6972

Located inside a private home, Gallery 2514 offers intimate, sporadic shows from the New Orleans visual art underground. The best time to check it out is during the monthly St. Claude Arts District evening open house.

Good Children

Bywater, 4037 St. Claude Ave., 504-975-1557; goodchildrengallery.com

This laidback collective gallery features high art with personality, and often a sense of humor as well. The collective includes the duo **Generic Art Solutions (GAS),** who have enacted a performance piece called "**Art Cops**" in the more highfalutin local art world arenas, handing out tickets for bad art and other offenses. Saturday and Sunday, 12 to 5 p.m., and special nighttime.

Home Space

Marigny/St Roch, 1128 St. Roch Ave., 917-584-9867

A casual space intermittently open for local art shows and other community gatherings (i.e. drinking events). Expect everything from photography and paintings, to original clothing and sculpted soaps. Call for hours or a private tour.

ARTS

The Oyster Factory

Treme, 1731 N Rampart St.,
504-616-5728; oysterfactory.org

The Oyster Factory opened concurrently with **Prospect 1**, the monster citywide art biennial that debuted in 2008. The space is a community-run visual art and performance collective, and focuses on folk and outsider art from the Gulf South.

JT

Rusty Pelican Art

Bywater, 4031 St. Claude Ave., 504-
218-5727; rustypelicanart.com

Out of their big beautiful funky St. Claude home right next to Goodchildren Gallery, the artists **Travis** and **Lexi Linde Wolf** fix motorcycles and other vehicles, and then make giant birds and other sculptures out of the leftover parts. A pretty funky, fun little place.

Sidearm Gallery

....

Marigny/St. Roch, 1122 St. Roch Ave., 504-218-8379; sidearmgallery.org

This community-based not-for-profit collective hosts avant-garde performance art, theatre, dance, fashion shows and film as well as visual art on the Marigny end of the St. Claude Avenue arts district (which means if you're gallery-hopping on the other end of the avenue, where art spaces are more densely distributed, you'll need a bike or car to get here). Opened in 2003, it was one of the earliest art spaces to open along the now-vibrant St. Claude strip.

A TOUR OF JULIA STREET ARTS DISTRICT

Some locals feel Julia Street's art is too safe. The free booze that once flowed down Julia during its annual **White Linen Night** *(first Saturday in August) and other events, has recently been stemmed to a slow trickle by the line you now stand in to buy drink tickets. (You then stand in another line for drinks; another impetus for the St. Claude Arts District). Zack Smith, though – our man on the inside – has high hopes and a positive attitude about Julia St., and is happy to give you, our readers, a tour. Most of the following galleries (and the other more craft-oriented spaces we've omitted)* are open Tuesday through Sunday, or else by appointment:*

LeMieux

323 Julia St. 504-522-5988;
lemieuxgalleries.com

"**Denise Berthiaum** began this gallery on Julia about 20-odd years ago; she was one of the first on Julia, when this place was scab alley, drunks, bad news, drugs being done in the alley. LeMieux shows very established, high-priced, interesting contemporary art."

Soren Christensen

400 Julia St., 504.569.9501;
sorengallery.com

"This one's been on the block a while. *(Looks in the window)* We're right now looking at some sort of pop renderings of Marilyn Monroe, and some photorealism."

Jonathan Ferrara

400a Julia St., (504) 522-5471;
jonathanferraragallery.com

"Ferrara is a vibrant fellow, and an artist himself. He's been around a long time in other locations and just moved to Julia. He shows a lot of artists that he has stuck with for years like **Dan Tague** (of **Good Children Gallery**) and **Miranda Lake,** one of his better-known artists."

Arthur Rogers Gallery

432 Julia St., 504.522.1999;
arthurrogergallery.com

"Along with LeMieux and **Steve Martin Gallery**, Arthur Rogers is one of the anchors of Julia. He's a well-established,

very respected collector. This stuff in here now is ten to fifty thousand dollars. At 434 Julia he has his annex – he's so big he needs two pairs of pants."

Heriard Cimino Gallery

440 Julia St., 504-525-7300;
heriardcimino.com

"This place shows nationally established mid-career artists: a lot of sculpture, but also painting, photography and installations of all styles." (*note: The website states that they "represent primarily New York and Miami based artists. Also prominent Louisiana artists."*)

Gallery Bienvenu

518 Julia St., 504.525.0518;
gallerybienvenu.com

"Pretty well known international artists and locals like **Raine Bedsole** who does paintings on boat oars. They have a lot of sculptures, installations and mixed media."

Jean Bragg Gallery of Southern Art

600 Julia St., 504-895-7375;
jeanbragg.com

"Specializing in 19th and 20th century Louisiana paintings, Newcomb College Pottery and Crafts, and **George E. Ohr Pottery**, the gallery also publishes and carries a wide range of books on the art of the South, including her own *New Orleans Arts District* magazine *(www.artneworleansmag.com)."*

Steve Martin Fine Art

604 and 624 Julia St., 504-566-1390; stevemartinfineart.com

"Shows other artists but mainly his own wire sculptures and paintings. Both he and Jean Bragg are stalwarts, movers and shakers of New Orleans' arts, who both fought to get tax exemption for any non-reproducible artwork sold on Julia Street. That was passed last year."

GSL Art Projects

614 Julia St., 504-508-2035

"GSL discovers and nurtures contemporary cutting edge New Orleans, and also promotes cultural exchanges between local and international artists and galleries."

George Schmidt Gallery

626 Julia St., 504-592-0206; georgeschmidt.com

"Schmidt is a prolific local artist who shows only his own work: primarily historical scenes on large canvases, very detailed." (*Authors' note: 35 years ago, Schmidt also co-founded the vaudevillian* **New Leviathan Oriental Foxtrot Orchestra**, *which has performed at more consecutive Jazz Fests than any other band. Also, his website bio is very entertaining*).

Michelle Y Williams Gallery

835 Julia St., 504.585.1945; michelleywilliams.com

"Exclusively features Williams' abstract paintings on canvas, metal, Plexiglas and wood, in acrylic, oils and often, raw materials such as sand."

OTHER NEIGHBORHOODS' ART

Backstreet Cultural Museum

Lower 9th Ward, 1116 St. Claude Ave., 504-303-9058; backstreetculturalmuseum.org

Located in New Orleans' Seventh Ward (just a hop from the Quarter, though you may not want to go on foot) the Backstreet Cultural Museum is the genuine article. The museum's holdings, curated by "self-motivated historian" **Sylvester Francis**, is an overflowing repository of artifacts documenting New Orleans' amazing African-American urban cultural traditions. Items from the museum are shown each year on the grounds of **Jazz Fest**, but it's better to dig them in their home, in the historic Treme. It's a unique window into the venerable worlds of Mardi Gras Indians, Social Aid & Pleasure Clubs, traditional jazz funerals and Mardi Gras groups like the **Northside Skull and Bones,** and **Baby Dolls**. On Mardi Gras Day, it's a good place to spot some downtown Mardi Gras Indians out showing off the pretty.

House of Dance and Feathers

Treme, 1317 Tupelo St., 504-957-2678; houseofdanceandfeathers.com

The beautifully named House of Dance and Feathers is a tribute to New Orleans' urban cultural groups, specifically Mardi Gras Indians and Social Aid and Pleasure Clubs, and the social history of the Lower Ninth Ward. The museum was started as a personal archive (and barbershop) in a backyard shed. Curated by **Ronald Lewis**, a former streetcar repairman and union rep, the collection was completely rebuilt after Hurricane Katrina and now does double duty as a meeting spot for community organizers working to rebuild the neighborhood. In 2009, Lewis and the excellent documentary/education group the **Neighborhood Story Project** (see *Literary New Orleans section*) published a full photo catalog and history of the museum. Call for an appointment.

The Big Top

·······································

Uptown, 1638 Clio St., 504-569-2700; 3ringcircusproductions.com

The Big Top is a multi-purpose gallery space, operated by the **Three Ring Circus** arts collective, just over the border into what locals refer to vaguely as Uptown – upriver of the business district in a part of town where not much goes on after dark except the **Circle Bar.** Still, it's a worthwhile spot to see quirky local art, theater and bands in a nonsmoking venue (they also do yoga classes and often, a Friday-afternoon music "camp" for kids, with cocktails for grownups) and during Mardi Gras season, its location just off the St. Charles Ave. parade route makes it a hopping home base for marathon bead-catching.

Dr. Bob's Art Gallery

·······································

Bywater, 3027 Chartres St., drbobart.net

If, during the course of your visit to New Orleans, you do something like eat in a restaurant, drink in a bar, or shop in a store, the odds are you'll see a quaint, hand-painted sign with a bottle-cap frame that says "Be Nice or Leave." These are the work of Dr. Bob, a local character and self-styled folk artist whose Ninth Ward warehouse is almost always open to the public. Visit as much for his personality as for the color-splashed, rough-hewn art.

The Pearl Gallery

*Uptown, 4421 Magazine St.,
504-322-2297*

Not to be confused with the bizarre Ninth Ward speakeasy of the same name, Uptown's Pearl is a recent addition to the Magazine Street corridor. Their latest show, at press time, featured the lowbrow rock n'roll poster-style work of local artist **Stevie Williams**.

Poets Gallery

*Uptown, 3113 Magazine St.,
504-899-4100*

This framing shop shows local artists with a decidedly goth bent, like **Hazard County Girls** front-gal **Christy Kane** – who makes creepy, delicate Victorian-looking dolls – and **Chris Slave**, whose canvases depicting New Orleans scenes are awash in rich, jewel-like swirls of deep, dark color.

N.O. MOMENT:

OGDEN AFTER HOURS

WEEKLY MUSIC SERIES AT
OGDEN MUSEUM OF SOUTHERN ART

*CBD, 925 Camp St., 504-539-9600
ogdenmuseum.org/education/ogden_after_hours*

JT

This weekly music event, which takes place on Thursdays from 6 to 8p.m. is popular with the after-work, white-wine-in-plastic-cups crowd. Southern musicians play two short sets broken up by a twenty-minute interview conducted by a local music writer. Once a month, the **Ponderosa Stomp** (see *Festivals*) sponsors the event, so there's a one-in-four chance you'll see a ninety-year-old blues or soul legend playing the museum lobby and sharing some amazing life stories. It's low on rock factor, but the interviews are a nice extra and it's a good way to see a lot of New Orleans music in a short weekend visit.

N.O. MOMENT:

THE GREY GHOST: ANTI-ART

*"The Grey Ghost is haunting my hood /
But I don't think his graffiti's very good"*

'The Grey Ghost,' by Miss Pussycat and Quintron

A plethora of "street art," much of it not very ambitious, can be found in and around New Orleans. The famous muralist Banksy even came down during one of our hurricane evacuations and left some presents for us upon our return (look for the girl holding the umbrella just outside the Quarter, where Rampart St. meets St. Claude). But in recent years, the sheer amount of graffiti has doubled in both amount and ambition, thanks to one of the city's more peculiar "artists." Fred "Grey Ghost" Radtke gets his name from the dull, industrial color of paint he uses to roll over the work of every other graffiti artist in the city. And it's not just errant art he despises; Radtke slathers grey over lost dog fliers, heavily stickered stop signs, and in more than a few instances, commissioned artwork on private property. Our professional opinion? Dude's nuts. You'd think art killed his mama. But an overwhelmed and overburdened city government praised his vigilante efforts – which he masks with a non-profit organization called "Operation Clean Sweep" – and in turn gave Radtke a huge sense of entitlement. But rather than quiet his rivals, Radtke's broad canvases of gray have ironically encouraged and inspired more graffiti than ever, especially in the post-apocalyptic period after Katrina. Over the past several years this back-and-forth has turned into a culture/art/street war and a fascinating visual conversation, violent at times (a claim both sides have made), but mostly entertaining. One of Banksy's aforementioned evacuation works depicted old sour-faced Radtke in a rocking chair, waving a tiny American flag, until Radke of course grey-ed it out. You'll probably even see Radtke's face stenciled over some of his own work by a wry artistic responder, with a word balloon begging to be filled.

DAN FOX

Fair Folks and a Goat

Marigny, 2116 Chartres St., 504-872 9260; fairfolksandagoat.com

The New Orleans branch of a Manhattan art boutique. Hang out, lounge, sip coffee on furniture you're welcomed to buy. Check out local books, the work of neighborhood clothing designers, and intermittent quieter shows by Bywater/Marigny musicians.

Trouser House

Bywater, 4105 St. Claude Ave. , 504-626-3653; trouserhouse.org)

From the website: "Trouser House is a contemporary art and urban farming initiative that promotes a model of sustainability defined by community involvement and public education. As a catalyst for social change, we advocates food activism and contemporary art as vehicles for improving public health and personal well-being." They also host art shows.

X/O Studios

Bywater, 2833 Dauphine St., 504-949-8134; videos.nola.com/times-picayune/2008/06/xo_studios.html

13 rooms of Local Art. Hours Wed-Sat 10am to 5pm and by appt.

WHAT OTHER PEOPLE WILL TELL YOU ABOUT

The big guns, mostly – which are perfectly legit. **The Ogden Museum of Southern Art** (*925 Camp St., 504-539-9600; ogdenmuseum.org*) has a great collection of contemporary and classically important pieces from below the Mason-Dixon. **The New Orleans Museum of Art (NOMA)** (*Esplanade Avenue at City Park, 504-658-4100; noma.org*) holds its own against any national museum, and is in a nice park. And the **Contemporary Arts Center (CAC)** (*900 Camp St., 504-528-3805, cacno.org*) hosts a cool, eclectic year-round program of films, music and events hosted amid their fine permanent collection.

TATTOOS

Veteran guitarist **Tony Barton**, late of psych-rap act **MC Trachiotomy** and R&B grunge group **The Special Men**, opened **Hell or High Water Tattoo Shop** (*Uptown, 2035 Magazine 504-309-5411*) in September of 2009. "Mine is more of an old-style New Orleans street shop," says Barton, a Louisiana native. "We do appointments but also walk-ins." His artists vary in style. "They cover all the bases: **Daniel Barre**, **Jimmy The Saint** (of heavy rock band **Endall**) are I are more neo-traditional, with a new school edge. **Jordan Barlow** (who plays in black metal band **Ritual Killer**, and has an eagle inked on his forehead) does more realistic portraits, all evil black and gray shit. **Eric Huffman** does straight traditional old-school, looks like it came from the 50's, with simple shading and bold outlines." Hell or High Water is open every day from 11am to 11pm. But if something worse than high water or hell has them closed during your visit to New Orleans, Barton suggests his impressive competition:

Electric Ladyland
....
Marigny, 610 Frenchmen St., 504-947-8286; electricladyland.net

Located among Frenchmen's many awesome music clubs, this is a real clean, laid back den of talented people, named "Best place to get a tattoo," by Gambit Weekly ten times.

Tattoo Gogo
....
Uptown, 4421 Magazine St., 504-899-8229; tattooagogo.com

This art-focused custom shop draws designs for each client. The school-educated artists vary in style from traditional to Americana to Japanese.

Uptown Tattoo
....
Uptown, 575 S Carrollton Ave., 504-866-3859; uptowntattoos.net

Near the university, this place is old style traditional. Worth a visit just to see the attached machine shop, which creates fancy, handcrafted and custom built tattoo machines.

Guitarist Tony Barton, owner of
Hell or High Water Tattoos

NEW ORLEANS THEATRE AND DANCE

With all the actual drama around the city, of course New Orleans would also posses a thriving theatre scene. We've always been famous for our plays, and our dancing (in whatever odd form it takes). Here however, burlesque is taken as seriously as the Nutcracker, and roller derby may as well be Shakespeare. As with all other events in New Orleans, the dance scene strives to, above all, entertain; almost every entertainer in the city, no matter how self-serious, puts the crowd's pleasure on par with their own. Meaning, even the most "arty" or "post-modern" dance or theatre production here will likely be energetic, smart, and fun.

Burlesque is a respected artform in New Orleans

N.O. MOMENT:

New Orleans' Burlesque Tradition Lives On

Today, Bourbon Street is a, cheeseball adult amusement park of karaoke bars, corporate-owned strip joints, bars that sell giant go-cups shaped like headless naked ladies and expensive souvenir shops hawking T-shirts emblazoned with slogans like "Katrina Gave Me A Blow Job I'll Never Forget." Fifty or sixty years ago, though, the neon strip was... well, a *glamorous* adult amusement park populated by swank nightclubs where well-dressed couples hit the town to see **Sam Butera** at **Leon Prima's 500 Club**, and **Skip Easterling** and **Freddy Fender** with **Mac Rebennack** (a.k.a. **Dr. John**) at **Papa Joe's**. They also went to see burlesque: **Governor Earl Long's** paramour **Blaze Starr**, **Lilly Christine the Cat Girl**, **Tajmah the Jewel of the Orient** and the exotic green-haired **Kitty West** a.k.a. **Evangeline the Oyster Girl**, performing elaborate stripteases in opulent costumes backed by some of the city's hottest live bands.

The burlesque revival has recently hit critical mass across the U.S., with every town boasting a gaggle of girls in pasties and feather fans ordered from the Internet. New Orleans' renaissance scene began earlier than most, in the late '80s, when Oyster Girl Kitty West taught **Jane Blevin** her vintage routine. Local historian of the odd **Rick Delaup** also began his website, *www. eccentricneworleans.com* around then, compiling photos, interviews and footage of Bourbon Street ecdysiasts like **Linda Brigette** and **Wild Cherry**. Since the late '90s, the club at 615 Toulouse St. (*once the* **Shim Sham**, *now* **One Eyed Jacks**) has hosted its own house troupe. Today, several revivalist troupes exist in New Orleans and perform fairly frequently. Check their websites for show dates: **Reverend Spooky LeStrange's Billion Dollar Baby Dolls** (*www.myspace.com/billiondollarbabydolls*), **Bustout! Burlesque** (*www.bustoutburlesque.com*), **Fleur de Tease** (*www. fleurdetease.com*) In September 2009, Delaup also hosted his own burlesque festival: check his site for future dates. (*www. neworleansburlesquefest.com*)

A ballerina before moving to New Orleans in 2001, **Trixie Minx** didn't realize she wanted to dance burlesque until she evacuated for hurricane Katrina, and began to fear she might never get the chance. "I remember in my big heavy evacuation backpack," says Trixie, "I had no real change of underwear or clothes, just my pictures and journals and a pair of pasties that I was given, to learn how to twirl with." When finally allowed back into her city, Trixie founded **Fleur De Tease** burlesque variety show, who rock one Sunday night a month at **One Eyed Jacks**."Our themes are well-rounded," Trixie explains. "We are more of a vaudeville variety show, meaning not just girls getting naked but equal amounts fire, aerial acrobatics, hula-hooping, music and magic. And all of our girls are power players in the New Orleans burlesque community. Almost all of them have their own solo shows." Fleur De Tease member **Roxie LeRouge** also hosts the revolving monthly, **A Night at the Roxie**. **Natasha Fiore** and **Madame Mystere** run the **Storyville Starlettes** troupe, while aerialists **Sarah Bobcat**, **Niki Frisky**, and **Ooops the Clown** guide the **Mystic Pony Aerial Troupe**. FDT's kinkiest member, **Bella Blue**, founded the New Orleans School of Burlesque at Crescent Lotus Dance Studio (*3143 Calhoun Street, 382-5199*); seasoned students perform in the **Burlesque 101 Showcase** series at **AllWays Lounge**. This venue also plays host to Bella's **Dirty Dime Peep**

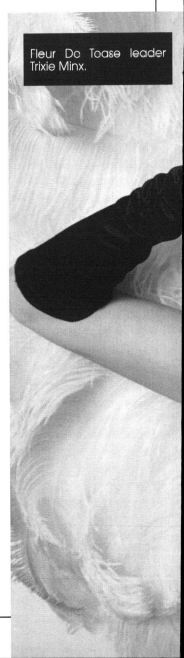

Fleur De Toase leader Trixie Minx.

Show which, Trixie ads, "Is way more naked than any other show in town, way more alternative."

Trixie herself can be seen, backed by a live band each Friday at midnight for free in the cast of **Irvin Mayfield's Burlesque Ballroom** (*French Quarter, Royal Sonesta, 300 Bourbon*). "The weekly Ballroom show is a modern take on a classic show, and a

very good introduction to burlesque, with live jazz from musicians such as **Meschiya Lake**, **Linnzi Zaorski**, **Jayna Morgana** or **Gerald French**."

If for some reason you miss Trixie while you're in town, she recommends other quality burlesque reviews. "There's a crop of young troupes that have only been around about a year, like **Crescent City Cupcakes** and **Kitty Glitter**. Most all of the troupes have home venues that dictate the style of the performance," Trixie explains. "Theatre shows tend to get more strange, almost performance art, while stuff in a rock club will have a more rock-n-roll vibe." More established acts include **Bustout Burlesque** (*bustoutburlesque.com*): "This is straight, classic burlesque with a live jazz band, once-a-month at House of Blues," Trixie says. "Bustout also puts on the **New Orleans Burlesque Festival** (*neworleansburlesquefest.com*) in late September, which brings in more national acts to share the stage with a few select local girls." **Slow Burn Burlesque** (*slowburnburlesque.com*) hosts once a month in the CBD at **Howling Wolf**: "Slow Burn are sort of neo-burlesque with a harder edge," says Trixie. "They do themed-shows, and often collaborate with rockin' bands like **Debauche**." Trixie also gives props to what she says is a group that has helped develop many of the current dancers in New Orleans' burlesque scene, "The Storyville Starlettes are the longest running troupe in town," she says. "many local girls were introduced to burlesque performance through them."

ARTS

All Ways Lounge/Marigny Theatre
....
Marigny, 2240 St. Claude Ave., 504-218-5778; marignytheatre.org

There's no telling what to expect at the strangest, nice new club in the Marigny. Once a Western-themed gay bar called Cowpokes, All Ways now hosts a beautiful music stage with a grand piano in the front room, and a small professional theatre for readings and intelligently bawdy plays in the back. The piano sometimes attracts fauxbeaux playing sepia-toned porch-stomp music, but with the right accordion and tuba combo, this is one place they can pull it off. During Mardi Gras and other busy times they'll even squeeze bands into a third outdoor performance area/atrium.

Anthony Bean Community Theater
....
Mid-City, 1333 South Carrollton Ave., 504-862-PLAY; anthonybeantheater.com

Community theatre in the truest sense. Anyone who's ever had theatrical ambition, people from the true crevices of New Orleans, come to light and shine in original productions tackling issues unique to the city. Not the flashiest thing to do on vacation, but you'll certainly get a glimpse into what New Orleans is really like.

ArtSpot

CBD, 6100 Canal Blvd., 504-826-7783, 866-ART-SPOT; artspotproductions.org

New Orleans is not big on modernity, or on thinking too hard in general, but **Kathy Randels** is an exception. In 1995, Randels founded ArtSpot, an ensemble of artists dedicated to creating original "meticulously LIVE theater" that blends and bends disciplines. Original multi-media works are co-developed among the cast, music is written, and rehearsals are painstaking and physical. ArtSpot also bolsters The LCIW Drama Club, a theatre company of inmates at The Louisiana Correctional Institute for Women in St. Gabriel, Louisiana, founded by Randels in 1996.

Ashe Cultural Arts Center

Uptown/Central City; 1712 Oretha Castle Haley Blvd., 504-569-9070; ashecac.org

Also a community gathering place and conference center, this performance space promotes African, Caribbean and African-American art and artists with frequent live concerts, dance recitals, movies etc.

The Backyard Ballroom

Bywater, 3519A St. Claude Ave., 504-473-6819; backyardballroom.com

The Backyard Ballroom is a theater project conceived by **Otter**, a flamboyant local performance artist with a marquee name in Ibiza clubland, and roaring flame tattoos on her personal orifices. Over the past year or so, she's re-imagined her sprawling 9th Ward mansion and the garden beside it into a funky performance venue for original musicals and theater written and performed by a collective of neighborhood artists. The end product is much more legit than our description belies.

Contemporary Arts Center (CAC)

CBD, 900 Camp St., 504 528-3800; cacno.org

This is no funky shotgun art shop. In two separate auditoriums and a main multi-room gallery, the CAC hosts music of all kinds – from brass bands, to avant orchestration, to huge bands like **Death Cab for Cutie** and **Ween** during JazzFest – plus theatre, local and national touring dance companies, and film festivals. $5 general, $3 students and seniors.11am to 4pm, Thurs. to Sunday.

ARTS

N.O. MOMENT:

MARDI GRAS INDIANS
THE DEEPEST AND MOST BEAUTIFUL NEW ORLEANS TRADITON YOU'VE NEVER HEARD OF

Mardi Gras Indians, resplendent in their intricately hand-beaded suits and headdresses weighed down with thousands of brightly colored feathers, are ubiquitous images in New Orleans' tourist materials. They're hired to parade through Jazz Fest to create ambiance, and since Katrina, nonprofits have subsidized

ARTS

ZS

Indian "practices" that are open to the public. These friendly presentations can contribute to a public image of the stalwart tradition bearers as sort of happy, colorful feathered friends. What most people don't talk much about is that Mardi Gras Indians can be some genuinely scary motherfuckers.

Locals say that the Indians – African-American groups divided into tribes that identify as either uptown or downtown-based – have been in effect since the 19th century. The tribal hierarchies include a Big Chief, a Big Queen and sometimes second and third chiefs and queens, plus the "spy boys," "flag boys" and "wild men." The tradition is interesting for combining aggressive, territorial hyper-masculinity with the domestic act of sewing; each man works all year to sew delicate, intricate patterns into a suit he will show off once or twice, before destroying it and starting over for next year. On Mardi Gras Day and **Super Sunday**, which falls in mid-March, the Indians don't parade so much as roam their neighborhoods, looking for other tribes for showdowns. Spy boys (you know the song) wander out ahead of the Big Chief to spot other tribes. These days, the contest is about who has the prettiest suit, but back in the day – especially on Mardi Gras Day, when confusion reigned in the streets and most people were masked – the battles were violent. As recently as the 90's, one Indian was allegedly nearly murdered by another looking to settle a score with him by a hatchet to the head. Some locals whisper that secret Indian Council meetings still have the power to decide life or death.

In the early 70's, members of the **Wild Magnolias** tribe, along with **Willie Tee**, recorded the first album of Indian songs ever put on wax (self-titled, but later put out with extra songs as *They Call Us Wild*) a deliciously raw and dirty slice of funk – one of the finest and most unique artifacts of genuine American music in existence – with the clattering tambourine and drum percussions the Indians use on actual runs.

On Mardi Gras Day or Super Sunday, neighborhood bars near Claiborne Avenue or under the Claiborne overpass (ie. Mother-in-Law Lounge) or Second and Dryades Streets, Bayou St. John and Treme are all great vantage points to catch the Indians' awesome spectacle. Or else all year round, you can visit the **House of Dance and Feathers** or the **Backstreet Cultural Museum** (see *Art Galleries*) to learn more about Indian history and custom.

DramaRama Performing Group

CBD, Contemporary Art Center, 900 Camp St., 504-528-3800; dramarama.org

This group curates an open-call mini-festival of all things theatrical (entry forms on their website), which for six hours in April, fills every inch of public space in the Contemporary Arts Center with new works of comedy, dance and theatre from nationally known artists, and most of the local dance/theatre companies detailed in this section. Its offshoot **DramaRama Junior** features new works by teenagers, while **DancerRama,** in March at the CAC, is a six-hour sampler platter of dancers from New Orleans and beyond.

Fringe Festival

venues all around the city, mostly in Bywater/Marigny, 504-941-3640; nofringe.org

A vast buffet of amateur and professional New Orleans performers producing, simultaneously all over the city, multimedia cabaret, comedy, dance, drama, magic shows, musical theater, performance art, puppetry, storytelling, burlesque, spoken word, you name it. The organization books all of the venues, rents all the chairs, handles all of the promotion, hires the volunteers, even buys the drinks, so that performers need only worry about their 30 to 60 minute performances. Entry forms on their website.

The Gong Show

pops up intermittently, usually at Hi-Ho Lounge, Bywater

Same rules as the regular gong show, except it's New Orleans "circus people," meaning clowns, fauxbeauxs, and players of old-timey instruments. The clowns perform mildly impressive but often-funny "tricks," or else just get naked and/or hurt themselves for everyone's entertainment. Expect to be thoroughly grossed out, but also laugh very hard.

Happensdance

offices at 129 University Pl., 504-523-6530

Founded by **Louisiana Philharmonic** cellist **Jeanne Jaubert**, this is one of those post-modern, experimental but fun dance troupes we mentioned.

Le Chat Noir

CBD, 715 St. Charles Ave., 866-597-5812; cabaretlechatnoir.com

The quintessential New Orleans theatre hosting mostly local productions from drama to retro cabaret, improvisational comedy, with a sprinkle of New Orleans' more theatrical music acts. Le Chat doesn't pander to the tourists, so it's generally not overrun with squares. Of course drinks are served.

Le Petit Theatre

French Quarter, 616 St. Peter St.,
504-522-2081; lepetittheatre.com

One of the nation's oldest continuously operating theaters. Meaning, it's beautiful but don't expect any envelope-pushing; they're slaves to schlocky musicals, and to Tennessee Williams – much of the **Faulkner** and **Tennessee Williams** festivals are held at Le Petit.

Louisiana Philharmonic Orchestra (LPO)

offices at 129 University Pl., 504-523-6530; lpomusic.com

The LPO is America's only musician owned and operated symphony – meaning they can play their classical music and pops favorites wherever they choose, from New Orleans' small First Baptist Church to the huge Morial Convention Center.

Mahalia Jackson Theater of the Performing Arts

Treme, 801 North Rampart St., in Armstrong Park, 504-529 3600; mahaliajacksontheater.com

Located inside **Louis Armstrong Park**, and named for the famous New Orleans born gospel star, this mainstream but beautiful theatre was creamed by Katrina and only reopened in January, 2009. Though famous as a place to hear opera and the Louisiana Philharmonic, the theatre also hosts mainstream Broadway fare like Cats and The Color Purple, plus a smattering of famous comedians and Black theatre productions.

The Mudlark

Bywater; 1200 Port St.
themudlarkconfectionary.com

This down-home crushed velvet hotbox of a theatre located on a flood-ragged street, features very small plays, puppetshows and other progressive performance and art, including a good deal of experimental and noise music.

New Orleans Ballet Association (NOBA)

Uptown/Garden District, 104 Dixon Hall, Tulane University,
504-522 0996; nobadance.com

Open from September to May at Tulane University's Dixon Hall, The NOBA Dance Institute is the largest dance classroom on the Gulf coast, providing thousands of recitals, concerts, lectures, workshops and classes. Check website for schedule.

New Orleans Ballet Theatre

various venues, 504-210-0222; nobt.org

This company's founders, **Gregory Schramel** and wife **Marjorie Hardwick**, danced in Miami, Cincinnati, Atlanta and Dallas, before returning to their home town. They claim as influences George Balanchine, Maurice Bejart and Twyla Tharp. Recent programs include the comedy "**Yes Virginia,**" and "**Thick as Thieves**" with music by U2.

New Orleans Center for the Creative Arts (NOCCA)

Marigny/Bywater, 2800 Chartres St., 504-904-2787; nocca.com

This school for creative high school students (which counts **Harry Connick Jr., Wynton** and **Branford Marsalis,** and **Terrance Blanchard** as its graduates, among many others) hosts performances of all kinds, from around the globe. Artists come to teach NOCCA students, and give stage performances that are open to the public. Ticket prices are also very reasonable.

New Orleans Opera Association

CBD, 1010 Common Street, Suite 1820, 504-529-3000; neworleansopera.org

The New Orleans Opera Association, founded as the French Opera House, is the oldest opera in North America. Performances are held at the Morial Convention Center and Tulane University's McAlister Auditorium.

Running With Scissors

norunningwithscissors.com

This newer but well-loved troupe presents mainly farce and high camp productions. Their performance locations vary from small theatres like Le Chat Noir to even bowling alleys, so check the website.

The Shadowbox

Bywater; 2400 St Claude Ave., 298-8676; theshadowboxtheatre.com

Among an increasing number of galleries and performance spaces on St. Claude, the intimate Shadowbox welcomes all types of shows from musicals to improv comedy by heady local troupe The New Movement.

Southern Repertory Theatre

French Quarter, 365 Canal St. 3rd Floor, 504-522-6545; southernrep.com

Just outside the French Quarter in what looks like a mall (because it is) Southern Reperatory. presents both classic and modern American and regional drama, featuring experienced local thespians as well as Broadway and Hollywood performers.

True Brew Coffee House

Warehouse District/CBD, 200 Julia St., 504-524-8441

This coffee shop is also a small theatre continuously hosting grassroots plays, poetry readings, improvisational comedy, cabaret, and of course music.

Tulane University's Shakespeare Season

Uptown, Lupin Theater, Tulane University, 504-865-5101

Shakespeare performances presented around the city in awesome park settings as well as on campus.

N.O. MOMENT:

THE BIG EASY ROLLERGIRLS

OTT
NTZ

Season runs almost all year around. Bouts take place at University of New Orleans' Human Performance Center, by Lake Pontchartrain, on the corner of Leon C. Simon and Elysian Fields; (www.bigeasyrollergirls.com)

The Big Easy Rollergirls – New Orleans' highly popular contribution to the now well-established national trend of that extreme girlie sport – describe their brand of flat track roller derby racing as "burlesque meets the X Games, meets WWE." They even have their own pinup calendar of big leggy blondes in short-shorts crashing against petite redheaded schoolgirls, and every other foxy female archetype on eight wheels.

The league consists of three teams: **The Confederacy of Punches**, **The Crescent Wenches**, and **The Storyvillians**. Several hundred New Orleanians fill the bleachers at the girls' brawls. A top-quality local rock band begins every event, and also provides entertainment for halftime, when most of the audience is drunk and howling for chick blood.

For the women, roller derby is not unlike being in a band – except way more work, with less drinking. The girls' intensely athletic practices occur early on weekend mornings, meaning the skaters can't really party much. If they miss practice, they're canned. The national Women's Flat Track Derby Association, of which the team is a satellite, also requires teams to complete a certain amount of community service hours. "We've cleaned up the lakefront," brags **Sally Asher** (skate name **SmasHer**) who plays "pivot" for the Confederacy of Punches. "We've polished statues in **City Park**, ran adoption drives for the Humane Society, you name it. We were even awarded a proclamation from the city for aiding the city's post-Katrina comeback."

On the days bouts occur, the ladies spend entire mornings and afternoons decorating the venue and laying down their own special track. Then they skate and fight at top energy for a couple of hours. And when the huge crowd finally leaves, having been totally rocked, the girls remove their skates to load everything back into the truck. All this to say: in no way is roller derby for wimps. Sit in the front row and maybe you'll get some of their hard-earned sweat on you.

Tsunami Dance Company

tsunamidance.com

Since 2002, this New-Orleans-based modern/multi-media dance company has incorporated athletic, innovative movement with a dynamic contemporary style. In fall 2008 Tsunami created an innovative, edgy take on **Bruno Schulz** imagery and philosophy for *Street of Crocodiles*. They can be seen at most of the events detailed in this section.

UNO Downtown Theatre

CBD, at the Scottish Rite Temple, 619 Carondelet St., 504-539-9580

Home to cutting edge and emerging theatre companies (**Running With Scissors, ArtSpot,** etc.) as well as UNO student and faculty productions.

Zeitgeist Multidisciplinary Arts Center

Uptown/Central City; 1724 Oretha Castle Haley Blvd., 504-525-6727; zeitgeistinc.net

Famous for their "theatre experiments," Zeitgeist, considered one of the premiere alternative arts centers in the South, also presents modern film, video, performance and visual art, and literary events six nights a week, year-round, plus many small "festival" type events in between. Support this amazing place!

NEW ORLEANS COMEDY

"Wild Man" Bill Dykes (facebook.com/billdykes) is one of New Orleans' few full-time working and touring comedians. In the mid 90's, Dykes joined the "Comedy Crew," made up of students from the University of New Orleans' first comedy course, "Intro to standup Comedy." The scene boasted folks like Ken Jeung, who famously quit his job as a dentist to perform in clubs and eventually win parts in The Hangover and other popular flicks. Dykes has produced shows at One Eyed Jacks and House of Blues, hosted the cable acces comedy show Blah Blah Blah with comic Fayard Linsey (who still does the show), and was the first comic after Katrina to set up a comedy night at Lucy's Retired Surfer Bar in the CBD. Called "the Godfather of New Orleans Comedy," by some, Dykes has been on three USO tours of Iraq and Quwait. "Currently, I live in a van by the river," says Dykes, meaning he's constantly on the road. "There is a whole new breed of open mic comedians in New Orleans though, that bring in strong audiences," he says. "Comedy in this city used to be more underground, but it's in the forefront now and more recognizable." Here are Dykes' suggestion for where you should go see comedy:

COMEDY VENUES

Carrollton Station (WEDS)

Uptown, 8140 Willow St., 504-865-9190; carrolltonstation.com

Every Wednesday at 8pm for seven plus years, **Mike Henehan** and **Scottland Green** have hosted "You Think You're Funny," a high-quality comedy open mic night. Packed audiences. Cheap drinks. Free entry.

Howling Wolf Den (THRS)

CBD, 907 South Peters St., 504-529-5844; thehowlinwolf.com/the-den/

Every Thursday, comedian **Red Bean** hosts "Comedy Gumbeaux" (comedygumbeaux.com). This comedy night with an urban edge features the best in the city, plus the occasional national star. 8pm.

ARTS

La Nuit Comedy Theatre (MON & FRI)

....

Uptown, 5039 Freret St., 231-7011; nolacomedy.com

Monday and Friday La Nuit hosts a standup open mic hosted by **Jonah Baschle**. The rest of the time it's mostly improv troupes, but they also host comedians and comic plays, even comedy classes for kids and adults.

Lost Love Lounge (TUES)

....

Marigny, 2529 Dauphine St., 504-949-2009; lostlovelounge.com

Not only great Vietnamese food, but on Tuesday night, **Cassidy Henehan** and **Scottland Green** host "Comedy Catastrophe," which usually starts late, 10:30pm at the earliest.

Road dog comedian "Wild Man" Bill Dykes

The Shadowbox

....

Marigny, 2400 St. Claude Ave., 298-8676; theshadowboxtheatre. com

Hosts various comedy events including "Megaphone Night," presented by **The New Movement** comedy troupe, which begins with a free improv class, continues with an improv jam open to all, and finishes with a professional comedy show. $5 entry, or free for those attending the class. The long form improv troupe **Awkward Headbutt** perform each Thursday night at 11pm for $10.

Yo Mama's (SAT)

....

French Quarter, 727 St. Peter St., 523-7469: nationalcomedycompany. com

For over 5 years the National Comedy Company has entertained visitors and locals just off of Bourbon St. across from **Preservation Hall** with its "Usual Saturday Night" improv comedy jam on, you guessed it, Saturdays.

ARTS

SHOPPING

No matter where you go, from San Francisco to Spain, the guidebooks always make it seem like buying things in a strange new place is one of life's more important cultural experience. We propose that when you visit New Orleans, it's better to first buy beers and food, and spend your time talking to people you meet and hearing live music. After that, however, here are some locally-owned shops that will supply you with souvenirs while also giving you a feel for the true nature of the city:

The Bargain Center Thrift store, across from Bywater Resturant and Deli.

THRIFT STORES AND COSTUME SHOPS

This is just the tip of the berg as far as places you can go to find costumes for Halloween, Mardi Gras, and any wild New Orleans event in between.

Bargain Center

....

Bywater, 3200 Dauphine St., 504-948-0007

Bargain Center is one of the coolest junk shops you'll ever visit. Everything from nice clothes to slightly damaged musical equipment to a comprehensive collection of Mardi Gras costumes and paraphernalia.

Cree McCree

....

Uptown, 3728 Laurel St., call for appt. 504-269-3982

Cree McCree became a professional flea in 1975, and has taken her cheap but wearable assemblage art, using found objects, garage sale finds and vintage hats, around the country. Author of the how-to guide **Flea Market America: The Complete Guide to Flea Enterprise** (available

on amazon.com), McCree also maintains the blog **Flea Queen of Planet Green**. Several times a year Cree opens her home to sell her own line of Halloween Cocktail Couture (bat bustiers, skeleton bras and vintage hats festooned with bats, spiders, ravens and snakes) plus fabulous Mardi Gras headpieces. Otherwise her wares can be found at **Freret St. Market** *(first Saturday monthly, September to June)*, **Broad St. Flea Market & Bazaar** *(second Saturday monthly, September to June)*, **Blue Nile Boo-tique** *(Sunday before Halloween)* and **Blue Nile Mardi Gras Costume Sale** *(Sunday before Mardi Gras)*.

Fifi Mahoney's

French Quarter, 934 Royal St., 504-525-4343; fifi-mahoney.com

Owned by **One Eyed Jacks** club owner **Ryan Hesseling** and his wife **Marcy**, Fifi's is a temple to all things glamorously over-the-top. Need a rhinestone ring the size of a doorknob? Perhaps a bubblegum pink wig covered in glitter, done up in a three-foot bouffant? Pancake makeup that'll cover your five o'clock shadow? A favorite of burlesque dancers, drag queens and Carnival revelers of all stripes, Fifi's is your spot.

Funky Monkey

Uptown, 3127 Magazine St., 504-899-5587

Divided into men's and women's sides, Funky Monkey sells gently used cool clothes and accessories of mostly recent vintage, plus some new pieces, sunglasses and costume jewelry. The men's side also prints T-shirts to order, or with logos of beloved local businesses like **K&B** (R.I.P.) and **Hubig's Pies**.

Le Garage

French Quarter, 1234 Decatur St., 504-522-6639

On the funky strip of Lower Decatur dominated by punk dive bars and service industry locals' favorite pubs, there are also several intriguing antique and junk shops of which Le Garage – so named because of its garage door that yawns open like Aladdin's cave – is one of the longest standing. They have a large stock of Carnival costumes, odd military surplus, plus various other quirky objects including movie posters, ceramics, and other treasures and relics.

Sole Starr Costumes

....

Bywater, 3000 St. Claude Ave., 504-948-4440

This is the sister store to **Sole Starr** boutique on lower Decatur Street in the Quarter, except it's not really a store. No words at all out front, just some spray-painted stars. The place is only "open" Wednesdays and Thursdays, plus all week before Halloween, and all through Mardi Gras season – still though, you MUST call first. If she's around, **Dee Dee** herself will invite you over and give you a private tour of costumes, tights, eyelashes, facepaint, stage blood, plus regular thrift wear, streetwear, vintage underwear and pseudo lingerie.

Trashy Diva

....

Uptown, 2048 Magazine St., 504-299-8777; and 829 Chartres St., 504-581-4555; trashydiva.com

Begun as a vintage shop in the French Quarter in the mid-90's, Trashy Diva is now the showcase for owner **Candice Gwinn's** lovely, retro-inspired dresses. Done in silk and more inexpensive cotton in a variety of mid-century-style prints, the designs are brand-new versions of the amazing 1940's and 50's-era styles that are now impossible to find, or cost a grand on eBay. There's also jewelry and a carefully curated selection of bags and shoes (Trashy is the only Frye shoe retailer in town). The French Quarter store also has a boutique dedicated to lingerie and corsets.

N.O. MOMENT:

Defend New Orleans Clothing Company

Defend New Orleans is not just a popular local clothing design. OK, it sort of was only that before the flood. Though even back then there was a need to guard the city from aggressive homogenizing forces. Soon after its inception, *Defend New Orleans* was adopted by the community as a symbolic mascot for the city's cultural preservation movement. Soon hundreds of bathroom mirrors, walls, and cop cars all bore the now-iconic Mohawk skull graphic.

After Katrina, as developers and national chains began moving in with apparent little care for the intricate history of the city, *Defend New Orleans* (run, admittedly, by an out-of-town transplant) stepped up as a subversive guerilla protest

DAN FOX

movement, and also simply as a celebration of the unique culture and warmth that exists here, alongside problems other US cities don't have. Imbued with a new, stronger meaning post-flood, *Defend New Orleans* garnered mad success – success they've shared with the community. Without any formal advertising or press, Defend raised over $10,000 in the fall of 2005 for the **New Orleans Musicians Fund, Habitat for Humanity, New Orleans Restoration Fund** and the **Association of Community Organizations for Reform Now (ACORN)**. Since then, money from the sale of Defend merchandise has also aided **Bridge House**, **Emergency Communities**, **Tipitina's**

Foundation, **New Orleans Musicians Fund**, and **Renew Our Music**, among others.

Defend New Orleans clothing can be purchased at various locations around town including Uptown at **Funrock`n**, **In Exchange**, **Funky Monkey**, **Peaches** record store in the Quarter, and also at DNO's website (*www.defendneworleans.com*), which doubles as a community sounding board, hipster video blog, music and events calendar, and ongoing documentary of the same particular (peculiar?) types of New Orleans culture featured in this guidebook.

MUSICAL INSTRUMENT SHOPPING

New Orleans has far less musical instruments stores than you'd expect, and none of our few choices is a vast shiny room gorged with brass. **Carlos McInerney** *owner of* **Allied Music**, *says that after Katrina, relief centers bought many young New Orleans high school marching band members free instruments.* **The Tipitina's Foundation** *(www.tipitinas.com) ongoing* **Instruments A-Comin'** *charity effort is one of the most prominent) Which is great for the schools, bad for the shops. So, visiting musicians, please patronize these independent music shops:*

Paul Webb, owner and proprietor of Bywater Music

JT

Allied Music

Mid-City, 4417 Bienville St., 504-488-2673; alliedmusic.net

Drumsticks, available at New Orleans' oldest music store, Allied Music.

Before the flood the oldest music store in New Orleans (est. 1966) had a bigger inventory . Now it's a little more plain-Jane – a very slim, basic collection of band stuff for sale, with a concentration on drums, as Allied's owner Carlos McInerney is also a passionate drummer and a partner in the **Crescent City Drum School** for kids.

International Vintage Guitars

CBD/Warehouse District, 646 Tchoupitoulas St., 504-524-4557

The foreign car dealership of music shops, you won't find many deals here but there is a lot of gear to drool over and it's all really well-maintained.

New Orleans Music Exchange

Uptown, 3342 Magazine St., 504-891-7670; dkclay-nola.com/ neworleansmusicexchange

With its stacks of speakers by the front door and rooms stuffed full of equipment, it's easy to get figuratively lost in this music shop. A constantly rotating stock of guitars, basses, drum sets, recording gear, brass instruments and DJ equipment is available for purchase, rental or trade. Owner **Jimmy Glickman** and his staff, who are all working and performing musicians, are (mostly) always happy to help, whether you're buying a guitar pick or a full backline.

SHOPPING

Webb's Bywater Music

....

Bywater, 3217 Burgundy St.,
504-232-5512

The first music store in recent mind to take up residence in the musicians' haven that is Bywater. Paul Webb – of semi-famous metal bands **Spickle** and **Hawg Jaw** – worked for many years for LA Music Exchange, which didn't fix guitars. Now at his own shop, Webb offers to do *anything* for any musician. We have a distinct memory of Webb, one Mardi Gras, dressed as Jesus, carrying an electric guitar he'd built, shaped like a raw wood crucifix – so, surely he could do whatever *simple* thing you needed. Noon to 6p.m. every day.

RECORD STORES

For a city that loves its music, New Orleans has very few record stores. The ones we do have are, of course, funky.

DAN FOX

The Domino Sound Record Shack in Mid-City specializes in vinyl and tapes – CDs too, but mostly only by locals. The shop also released the last vinyl 12" by Why Are We Building Such a Big Ship?

Domino Sound Record Shack

Mid-City, 2557 Bayou Rd.,
504-309-0871

In a small Rasta neighborhood in Mid-City, Domino Sound houses a well-curated selection of old LPs, cassette tapes, and local bands' releases. The owner is **DJ Prince Pauper**, arguably the city's best dub reggae selector.

Euclid Records

Bywater, 3401 Chartres St., 504-947-4348; www.euclidnola.com

This sister store to the famous shop in St. Louis boasts an extensive, well-curated and organized collection of pretty much every type of music. New and used vinyl, a gorgeous collection of hand-screened posters, a good selection of music books (such as this one) and a stage in the corner for free instore performances by great local bands (and sometimes secret afternoon shows by whoever's playing a big venue that night) make this one of the best record stores in town.

Jim Russell's Rare Records

Uptown, 1837 Magazine St., 504-522-2602; jimrussellrecords.com

Some people consider Jim Russell's, now in its 40th year, the last of the real record stores in New Orleans. Others

complain that it's too expensive and unorganized. Either way, they sell tons of records in every possible condition, from old New Orleans Zydeco to 60's psychedelia to brand new techno, hip-hop and rock. They also sell new and used turntables and other DJ equipment, blank reel-to-reels, picture-discs, famous New Orleans 45s, even video games of all eras. Monday through Saturday 11 a.m. to 5 p.m.

Louisiana Music Factory

210 Decatur Street; 504-586-1094; louisianamusicfactory.com

Though they do have a "metal" section, they don't sell rap, and mostly don't allow any of the non-traditional bands featured in this book to play the store's very fun, free, afternoon in-store concerts. But somehow we still dig Louisiana Music Factory for their vast, two-floor collection of (almost) all things Louisiana.

The Mushroom

Uptown, 1037 Broadway St., 504-866-6065; mushroomnola.com

This is the obligatory funky college record store. Bongs and black light posters, plus a fun selection of new and used music. Plus it's nearby **Audubon Park** and the daiquiri shop.

Nuthin But Fire

1840 N. Claiborne Ave., 504-940-5680; nuthinbutfirerecords.com

Proprietor **Sess 4-5**, also a rapper, got his start rhyming with 504 boys like the **L.O.G** and **Shine Baby** back in junior high. He graduated to slinging burned CDs out of his trunk, and just after Katrina, opened his bona fide storefront across from the North Claiborne Avenue exit ramp. Nuthin But Fire curates their own series of local rap CD compilations and carries a wealth of NOLA and other hip-hop treasure, from vintage bounce to the latest discs showing up on the urban charts. It's also a great spot to pick up flyers for relatively underadvertised New Orleans hip-hop shows. And ask him about **Industry Influence** (*www.industryinfluence.blogspot. com*), the networking event and show he throws down on the first Monday of every month with **Q93.3FM's** star **DJ Wild Wayne.** P.S.: Dudes are still slinging burned CDs out of the trunk of a car most days in the parking lot two blocks down. We suggest you buy them legally from Sess, but if you have an adventurous spirit, we can't stop you.

Odyssey Records & Tapes

CBD, 1012 Canal St.,
504-523-3506

Founded 28 years ago, Odyssey finally reopened after Katrina on Canal, amid tourist-focused T-shirt shops and ghetto-focused jewelers. The shop peddles mostly hip-hop vinyl and CDs. Great vintage local stuff can be found if you dig, as well as info about upcoming rap shows.

Euclid Records in Bywater: the best new record store in town.

Peaches Records & Tapes

French Quarter, 408 N. Peters St.,
504-282-3322

Store owner **Shirani Rea** has, most notably, been instrumental in the New Orleans rap and hip-hop scene since 1975, when she opened her original Peaches record store (which used to be a branch of the defunct national chain; the NOLA outpost, which keeps the original sign, is now indie, and as far as we know, the only one left) almost as an office and community center for everyone from **Mystikal** to **Souljah Slim** to the **Cash Money Crew**. The 90's queen of **No Limit Records, Mia X**, was supposedly discovered while working at Peaches. Katrina forced Peaches' relocation into the French Quarter, with a similar vibe, but now featuring live performances from local groups in the store's big picture window. Plenty of New Orleans basics on the shelves, plus a great selection of national hip-hop and DJ vinyl. Of interest to some might be the always-available complete discography of the peculiar "blues comedian" **Poonanny**.

Skully'z Records

French Quarter, 907 Bourbon St.,
504-592-4666;
myspace.com/skullyzrecordz

The best new record store in the city. And on Bourbon Street, of all places! Tiny little Skully'z nonetheless stocks a mountain of new and used vinyl, and is a great place to pick up releases by New Orleans' alternative musicians.

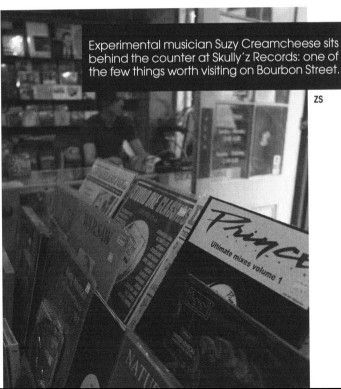

Experimental musician Suzy Creamcheese sits behind the counter at Skully'z Records: one of the few things worth visiting on Bourbon Street.

ZS

FRERET STREET
UPTOWN

thenewfreret.com

This historic street took on much water during Katrina but has bounced back to say the least. After some promised post-flood aid money failed to materialize, entrepeneurs in the area decided to rebuild their community themselves. Zoning as an arts and entertainment district allowed locals to start a weekly market that quickly brought a lot of positive attention to the area, along with a slew of independent, locally owned restaurants, bars and other shops. Aside from live music at the weekly market and the annual festival though, Freret hosts just one art gallery and one as-yet-to-be-opened live music club. Still, it's a great place to spend your money if you came here to shop. *AntiGravity Magazine* publisher **Leo McGovern** set up on Freret after Katrina in an office out of **Crescent City Comics** (*4916 Freret St.: crescentcitycomics.com*). Having watched the area bloom, Leo was our first choice to recommend Freret Street's best bets:

AntiGravity magazine publisher Leo McGovern of Crescent City Comics on Freret

Bloomin' Deals

4645 Freret St. 504- 891-1289; jlno.org

A huge consignment shop draped with new and used adult and children's clothing and shoes, housewares, furniture, books and more, run by The Junior League of New Orleans, an organization of women committed to developing the potential of women and improving communities through educational and charitable means. Meaning, tons of cool old-lady dresses!

Crescent City Comics:

Uptown, 4916 Freret St.; 504-891-3796

Without a doubt the best selection of comics and graphic novels in the city.

Du Mois Gallery

4921 Freret St., 504-818-6032

Nestled in a rambling shotgun, DuMois showcases regional mid-career and emerging talent in all mediums, with show openings on the second Saturday of each month from 5-8pm.

Freret Street Boxing Gym

4510 Freret St.; 895-1859

On many Friday nights this regular boxing gym becomes a huge partywhere everyone floods into the street to drink beer and watch amateurs slug it out ina professional ring. Obnoxious but super fun.

Freret Market

Intersection of Freret Street and Napoleon Avenue; freretmarket.org

Started in 2007, the market is a whole block of food, art, and flea. Local restaurants serve up unique dishes to the live local sounds of Alex McMurray, Lagniappe Brass Band, The Moonshiners and others, who all play close to the nice little kids area to accommodate groovy parents.

Freret Street Festival

Intersection of Freret Street and Napoleon Avenue; freretstreetfestival.com

The first Saturday of each month (except July and August). Over 200 local vendors and restaurants, four stages of local music (past years have included Big Sams Funky Nation, Tin Men, Debauche, Free Agents Brass Band). If the petting zoo in the elaborate "Kid Zone," isn't enough, the humane society also brings dozens of cute dogs and cats. Somewhere in there is usually some free rollerderby as well!

Village Tea and Coffee

5335 Freret St., 861-1909; villagecoffeeneworleans.com

The coffee might taste better somewhere else but this is a nice charming spot especially for college kids and they langniappe one chocoate espresso bean with your coffee order.

EAT AND GET DRUNK AT:

Beacoup NOLA

4719 Freret St., 504-430-5508;
beaucoupjuice.com

During the New Orleans summer, little stands pop up everywhere selling shaved iced drowned in colored high-fructose corn syrup. Beacoup NOLA is the first place to pour organic fruit juices on their snowballs. Smoothies, vegetable juice, even an assortment of paninia sandwiches are also available.

Cure

4905 Freret St., 504.302.2357;
curenola.com

Pricey little craft cocktail lounge for "mixology" fans and celebrity spotters.

Midway Pizza

4725 Freret St. 504-322-2815;
midwaypizzanola.com

Specializing in deep dish, Midway is the rare non-corporate pizza joint with a lunch buffet. Open till midnight.

Sarita's Grill Latin American Fusion Grill

4520 Freret St., (504) 324-3562

The owners are Cuban but the menu tackles all foods Latin from tacos to rice bowls to pressed sandwiches. Cheap but high quality.

MAGAZINE STREET

UPTOWN

Though we'd rather you focus on New Orleans music & art, there are a few lovely and highly walkable strips of shops here, of which Magazine Street Uptown is the most notable – for clothes, antiques, cool odds and ends and snacks. The businesses are almost all exclusively owned by New Orleanians. There are several definable chunks of Magazine Street where stores stand shoulder-to-shoulder, and the distance in between is safe to stroll and quite pretty. This path will also take you through the Garden District, heavily stressed in other guidebooks for its sprawling mansions, lush foliage and former residents **Trent Reznor** and **Anne Rice**.

Magazine Street is New Orleans' other shopping district outside the French Quarter.

DAN FOX

Aidan Gill

2026 Magazine St., 504-587-9090;
aidangillformen.com

A sort of manly beauty shop for the refined gentleman, **Aidan Gill** is a haven for men to repair to while their lady friends are in **House of Lounge** or **Trashy Diva**. The barbershop in the rear offers haircuts and hot towel shaves with a gratis Scotch on the rocks. The boutique in the front sells high-end shaving products (including bone-handled brushes and razors), cologne, cufflinks, ties and small books on etiquette and masculine pursuits.

Branch Out

2022 Magazine St., 504-371-5913;
branchoutshop.com

Branch Out is New Orleans' first "green" shopping alternative. Their sustainable clothing and accessories for men and women however, are more stylish than one would expect. This new and much-welcomed shop also carries hand-selected, quality vintage pieces and locally made designer goods – all green.

Dirty Coast

5704 Magazine St., 504-324-3745;
dirtycoast.com

New Orleans-themed T-shirts made by arty, graphically savvy people who also do a lot of local art-based community organizing sort of stuff. Their print styles are sort of reminiscent of the Urban Outfitters aesthetic, but depicting things like beignets, absinthe and jailbird former Louisiana Governor **Edwin Edwards**.

Earthsavers

5501 Magazine St., 504-899-8555;
earthsaversonline.com

This New Orleans mini-chain (there's another store in Metairie) has a focus on green products and living; they sell a line of organic cotton t-shirts whose proceeds go to various locally based eco-conscious rebuilding efforts. They carry most salon and upscale beauty lines, like Bumble & Bumble and Dr. Hauschka, and a chalkboard outside indicates which spa services are available for walk-ins.

Frock Candy

3112 Magazine St., 504-301-9864

Frock Candy makes their boutique eye candy by organizing their cute, cheap and super-trendy dresses by color, making the store into a fluffy jewel box that's somehow extra shoppable because of it.

House of Lounge

2044 Magazine St., 504-671-8300;
houseoflounge.com

Fancy-schmancy sexy underwear and stockings plus glamorous costume jewelry and a few naughtier selections, like sequined pasties and discreet, um, toys. HoL is designed like a luxe boudoir

SHOPPING

and carries everything from the sassy Jezebel line ($25 bras) to Aubade and La Perla's pricey scanties.

Neophobia

2855 Magazine St., 504-899-2444; neophobia-nola.com

This shop mostly carries mid-century furniture from names like Heywood-Wakefield, Knoll and other big guns of design, with mint-condition vintage glassware, dishes, magazines and clothes mixed in. Everything is in top-notch shape and priced accordingly.

The Reservoir

2045 Magazine St., myspace.com/thereservoir

This inexpensive but high-quality thrift and knick-knack store sells everything from pristine vintage kitchen appliances to clothes, records, jewelry, figurines and other cute nerd paraphernalia. If you want to feel a little better, just pop inside here.

Retro-Active

5414 Magazine St., 504-895-5054

This tiny shop is jam-packed with carefully selected mint-condition clothes, accessories and ephemera from the middle of the twentieth century. The collection of Bakelite and Lucite jewelry is especially impressive. No junk-shop bargains here, though; the owner has been in that spot for over a decade and is ridiculously knowledgeable about his collectibles.

Uptown Costume & Dancewear

4326 Magazine St., 504-895-7969

Great costume shop; the best, and also the busiest, place to go for Halloween and Mardi Gras shopping.

EAT AND GET DRUNK AT:

Bee Sweet

5706 Magazine St., 504-891-8333; beesweetcupcakes.com

A tiny storefront that sells giant cupcakes. The "Chubby Elvis" is a banana cupcake topped with peanut butter cream frosting (no bacon). All-natural "Pup Cakes" are also available for the dog.

Chez Nous Charcuterie

5701 Magazine St., 504-899-7303; gotocheznous.com

Despite a huge, ginormous Whole Foods Market across the street, tiny Chez Nous – located in a shotgun house catty-corner to the superstore – plugs away selling its own wines, gourmet and prepared foods. Daily menus showcase local ingredients and New Orleans-style dishes.

Joey K's

3001 Magazine St., 504-891-0997;
joeyksrestaurant.com

This stick-to-your ribs diner is a neighborhood institution for home-style New Orleans soul food. Think po-boys, fried soft-shell crab, and split pea soup with smoky slabs of bacon, oven-roasted turkey with stuffing and homemade bread pudding with ice cream for dessert.

Juan's Flying Burrito

2018 Magazine St., 504-569-0000;
4724 S. Carrollton Ave., 504-486-9950; juansflyingburrito.com

This punk-rock burrito shop stuffs huge California-style burritos for cheap with loud rock n'roll in the background and lowbrow local art on the walls. There's a branch on Carrollton Avenue in Mid-City which lacks some of the hipster appeal of the original.

Lilette

3637 Magazine St., 504-895-1636;
www.liletterestaurant.com

Simultaneously fancy and casual French bistro. Huge selection of unique and adventurous gourmet options. Open for lunch.

Ms. Mae's

4336 Magazine St., 504-895-9401; myspace.com/msmaes

Ms. Mae's is not only open 24-hours, but they have $1 drinks and beers AT ALL TIMES. They don't have an official Web page, but they do have a "Wall of Shame" site featuring photos of people who have fallen victim to their dangerous drink special: *msmaeswallofshame.blogspot.com*.

Sucre

3025 Magazine St., 504-520-8311;
shopsucre.com

If you want to eat a tiny cake that's covered in glitter, this is the place. It's a pastel-and-marble Parisian gem of a café that sets out delicately crafted chocolates, gelato and pastries (with a fondness for edible color and sparkle) as if they were priceless art.

Tee Eva's

5201 Magazine St., 504-899-8350
evapralines.com

Good sno-balls and tasty pies and praline candy. Try the miniature pies – pecan, sweet potato, or Creole cream cheese just enough for a snack. Mon. through Sat. 11a.m. to 6p.m.

PARKS AND OTHER FAMILY FUN

Some of New Orleans' parks are very elaborate and fun (and sell booze) while other are simple places to lay in the grass and chill (and drink booze). Or else ride horses, paddle canoes, and other forms of relaxing play.

Esteemed New Orleans photographer (responsible for our book's back cover photo) Shannon Brinkman and her daughter watch the Happy Talk Band at the Mirliton Festival in Bywater.

Audubon Park

Uptown, 6500 Magazine St., 1-866-ITS-AZOO; auduboninstitute.org

Designed by the same fellow who did Central Park, this bird-oriented jogging park (where people ride horses!) leads you around a beautiful moat full of giant white egrets, ibis, and other feathered species. Or if captive animals are more your thing, there's a zoo, and **Cascade Stables**, where the kids can take a riding lesson, or just gawk at the show ponies.

City Park

Mid-City, 1 Palm Dr. [or, corner of Esplanade and Carrollton], 504-482-4888; neworleanscitypark.com

This grand old park, which houses the **New Orleans Museum of Art** (beside an amazing sculpture garden) and more beautiful horse training stables, is also the home to many gigantic oak trees – though not near as many as before Katrina. Also on the vast shady grounds: tennis courts, an old but operating mini-train, and the kiddy park Storyland, with its antique merry-go-round and miniature rollercoaster, among other rides (plus low-key to-go beers and drinks for the parents). At Christmas time, City Park lights up for *Christmas in the Oaks*, featuring acres of illuminated Christmas tableaux, some with hilarious Cajun themes. Also, hot buttered rum!

The Fly

Uptown, Riverview Dr., Audubon Park

In back of **Audubon Park**, this Uptown river levee, known as The Fly, hosts a series of picnic areas and sportsfields, where on nice days hordes of college students (i.e. cute girls in bikinis) play Frisbee, sunbathe, drink, and smoke weed. During mellower times it's one of the city's nicest breezy places (New Orleans don't get many breezes) to view the Mississippi, sip wine, and watch the giant barges float by.

Lafayette Square Park

CBD, 500 St. Charles Ave., 504-881-9861; lafayettesquare.org

A beautiful patch of foliage and public art amid New Orleans' tallest buildings. This is also where the free *Concert in the Park* series is held Thursdays in the Spring, as well as the *Harvest the Music* free concert series each Thursday in the Fall. Both series cater to more touristy notions of New Orleans music (you will almost surely hear "When the

Saints Go Marching In"), even though most concert attendees are locals just getting off work. If you're simply visiting however, it may be the best part of you and your kids' trip.

Markey Park

Bywater, corner of Royal and Louisa

The home of the **Mirliton Music Festival**, and the weekly Bywater art market, is also Bywater's dog park, where you can sip a bloody mary from **Marky's Bar** or **Bywater Resturant and Deli** around the corner, and maybe involve yourself in a punk rock kickball game. There's also a pretty large, new, padded playground.

Washington Park

Marigny, corner of Frenchmen and Royal

This 'no dogs allowed' park functions as the Marigny's official dog park. Go figure. Along with some intermittent small literary and music fests (**Saints and Sinners Literary Fest** in May, **PrideFest** in June, see *Literary New Orleans*), and truly interesting public art (including **Marcus Brown's** interactive sound sculpture, HUMS), one can also witness fauxbeauxs practicing juggling, hula-hoop tricks and other mild acrobatics.

FUN FOR THE WHOLE FAMILY

Do we recommend you bring your kids to New Orleans? Yes, if 1) you've already been here at least once before to enjoy it as an adult, and 2) you're O.K. with not getting as drunk as that time, and 3) if the only time you flash folks is when you're breastfeeding. If you meet these requirements then, yes, your kids can get as much of a kick out of this weird crazy place as you do – if your trip is tightly curated. Here's a head start:

Algiers Ferry

French Quarter, at the foot of Canal St. next to the Aquarium

Since 1827, the Algiers ferry has conveyed folks across the Mississippi to Algiers Point, a quiet but fun neighborhood of beautiful New Orleans architecture, sans wild nightlife or much crime. This 15-minute scenic budget cruise on the River features a panoramic view of the city and costs $1 for cars. Free for bikes and pedestrians.

Aquarium of the Americas

French Quarter, 1 Canal St., 504-565-3800; auduboninstitute.org/aquarium

Not a very New Orleansy thing to do on your trip to New Orleans, since every city that wants tourist action has one. Still, ours is pretty nice, with a focus on Gulf Coast wildlife – you can't argue with albino alligators and giant sharks. To mom and/or dad, we recommend hitting the downstairs IMAX snackbar at the start of your aquarium tour, so you'll have a daiquiri to sip while walking around.

Audubon Insectarium

CBD, 423 Canal St., 504-410-BUGS; auduboninstitute.org/insectarium

This insect attraction opened in 2008 has been heartily embraced by New Orleans parents. Along with learning about bugs, you can touch some, walk among them in a butterfly garden, even eat crispy Cajun crickets and grasshopper chutney in the Critter Café. Just don't lead off with, "Hey kids! Wanna go eat bugs?!" Closed on Mondays.

Faubourg Marigny Home Tour

Mid May, starts at Washington Square Park, 700 Elysian Fields, 888-312-0812; faubourgmarigny.org

This big, fun self -guided walking tour lets you into the Marigny neighborhood's most magnificent historic and post-Katrina renovated homes and gardens. The event starts at 10a.m. with a kids' activity area (kids under 12 tour free) and an art market showcasing local art, photography, jewelry, home furnishings and more. The tour now also stops in the **Den of Muses,** where visitors can see colorful and bawdy floats being made and painted. Tickets are $15 in advance.

Freret Street Festival

Intersection of Freret Street and Napoleon Avenue; freretstreetfestival.com

The first Saturday of each month (except July and August). Over 200 local vendors and restaurants, four stages of local music (past years have included **Big Sams Funky Nation, Tin Men, Debauche, Free Agents Brass Band**). If the petting zoo in the elaborate "Kid Zone," isn't enough, the humane society also brings dozens of cute dogs and cats. Somewhere in there is usually some free rollerderby as well!

Imagination Movers (rock band for kids!)

check website for dates and venues: imaginationmovers.com

This Emmy nominated, primary colored rock band for kids can be seen on Disney TV and heard on Disney Radio. Imagination Movers concerts teach kids fun dances and games, and blow their friggin minds. Parents will be impressed by how hard "The Movers" actually rock, on modern-day classics like "The Medicine Song," "What's in the Fridge?" and "I Want My Mommy (Time for Bed)." These days the band can be seen on national television far more often

then at home, but check the website while you're in town.

Louisiana Children's Museum

CBD, 420 Julia St., 504-523-1357; lcm.org

Smack in the middle of the Julia Street Arts District, this 30,000 square foot playground for kids' bodies and minds is an essential part of any child's visit to New Orleans. Among a million other things LCM offers a kids' spelunking wall, astronomy demonstrations, a miniature New Orleans grocery store, live children's music, plus continuous art and music classes and other special events such as Winnie the Pooh's birthday, done New Orleans style.

Mardi Gras World

West Bank, 233 Newton St., 504-361-7821; mardigrasworld.com

The ferry mentioned above takes you pretty darn close to Mardi Gras World, where all of Carnival's mainstream floats are built, at the incredibly colorful outsized studio of **Blaine Kern,** the world's leading makers of float sculptures and props. Giant grinning heads, giant mythological beings, giant crabs and crawfish – everything GIANT. As close as a kid may come to Charlie's Chocolate Factory, and pretty interesting if you don't know much about Mardi Gras (or have never worked in a float den for $8-an-hour).

Musée Conti Wax Museum

....

917 Rue Conti , 504-581-1993, or 800-233-5405;
neworleanswaxmuseum.com

Founded in 1963, Musee Conti tells the story of 300 years of New Orleans history from her founding to the present day, via 154 life-size figures displayed in historically accurate settings.

New Orleans Hornets

....

CBD, New Orleans Arena,
1501 Girod St., 504-587-3663;
neworleansarena.com

October through April, watch New Orleans' own NBA team (with it's cool hornet-as-fleur-de-lis logo) shoot hoops at the New Orleans Arena. Tickets range from $15 to $1,700.

N.O. MOMENT:

NEW ORLEANS SAINTS (NFL FOOTBALL)

Win or lose (since Superbowl XLIV...win) New Orleanians love dem **Saints**, our formerly beleaguered boys in black and gold. To give them credit, they've done a lot better since the flood. Plus, games are a huge excuse to party NOLA style. Outside of the completely refurbished **Superdome** you'll be swept up in a parade of football-frenzied fans, some in elaborate costumes (perhaps even an odd character in Saints garb trying to rile the crowd while circling the Dome in a flat-bed truck) almost all with beer and daiquiris. Inside, you'll be treated to impromptu performances by jazz bands that roam the stands, and a crowd that so completely understands what it means to lose that its ability to celebrate victory is unparalleled. Add in a ticket price below the NFL average, plus the cheapest beer in the league and you win, whether or not the Saints do.

Ripley's Believe it Or Not Museum

....

French Quarter, 620 Decatur St., 504-586-1233

Wax statues and other replications of phenomena you may or may not believe to be true.

Summer Stages

....

CBD, 225 Baronne St., 504-598-3800; summerstages.org

A theatre featuring a wide array of contemporary musicals and other original New Orleans productions for child performers.

Zephyr Baseball

....

Metairie, 6000 Airline Dr., 504-734-5155; zephyrsbaseball.com

From April to August, watch New Orleans' baseball team play – not in the city but in the not-far-away burbs of Metairie. Tickets are cheap, with lots of special deals and giveaways.

FAMILY FUN

JT

OTHER PLACES ARE INTERESTING TOO:

They're not evacuating, they're just taking a "daytrip"!

DAYTRIPS JUST OUTSIDE NEW ORLEANS

The combination of Louisiana's temperate weather and vibrant regional culture means that throughout the lengthy Spring/Fall, each weekend offers a multiplicity of food and music festivals and other attractions within a day's drive of New Orleans. Festing goes on year-round, really, but on a good May or October weekend it's possible to hit three or four good ones on less than half a tank of gas. And the French Quarter has nothing on those people in regards to music and food. The 'burbs also host some amazing markets and shops. Here are a few fun places you can go for an afternoon, a day, or if you're forced to evacuate:

Dorignac's Food Center

Metairie [just over the parish line from downtown New Orleans], 710 Veterans Blvd., 504-834-8216; dorignacs.com

Going to a grocery store doesn't sound like much of a field trip, but in the afternoon, Dorignac's bakery and seafood deli are both stacked with French breads and fresh shrimp and homemade crabcakes and remoulade – plus an insane wholesale booze selection, from European-priced wines that taste great, to a thousand kinds of vodka in an icy wonderland of over-ambitious bottle designs. If you're having a cookout in New Orleans, or maybe thanking the friends whose floor you're staying on by cooking a meal, Dorignac's is pretty much the New Orleans equivalent of the meat, cheese, and booze markets of France and Spain. 7am to 9pm every day.

Jefferson Flea Market

Jefferson Parish [a few miles from downtown New Orleans], 5501 Jefferson Highway, 504-733-0011

The flea market, open on weekends only, has long been the go-to spot for inexpensive antique furniture for New Orleanians (particularly armoires, since because of strange taxation laws, traditional New Orleans shotgun houses don't have closets. So if you want an armoire, New Orleans is a good place to get one. We have lots). Anyway, the many booths in the flea market complex are also full of more portable curiosities, many with local flavor; World's Fair souvenirs and promotional items bearing the names of beloved but defunct New Orleans brands like **K&B** drugstore, **Jax** and **Regal** beer, **Krauss** and **Maison Blanche** department stores are all still in steady supply.

Daytrips

Jefferson Variety

Jefferson [a few miles from downtown New Orleans], 239 Iris Ave., 504-834-2222; jeffersonvariety.com

You say there's no reason you can think of to have to visit a fabric store on vacation? Apparently, you've never been to New Orleans, where parties, parades, festivals and other various and sundry occasions demand a costume. And Jefferson Variety, with its rainbows of costume satin, yards of shimmering taffeta and what looks like endless miles of strips of braided sequins, rhinestones and multicolored fringe, will make you want to find a reason. It's also where, they claim, Mardi Gras Indians buy their feathers, and big-time Carnival krewes buy the elaborate sequined appliqués and fake stones that give their royal robes sparkle.

Louisiana Crawfish Festival

four days and nights at the end of March, Chalmette, LA [nine miles east of New Orleans,] 337-332-1414; louisianacrawfishfestival.com

St. Bernard Parish, home of the Battle of New Orleans site overlooking the Mississippi River, also hosts the Crawfish Fest (est. 1975). For the uninitiated, crawfish (a.k.a. crayfish, crawdads, mudbugs) are pretty much poor man's shrimp. They take a lil' more work to peel, and the meat's small, but totally worth it – not to mention that crawfish bring people together, creating a whole other party scene during the winter festival season. Aside from your basic boiled crawfish, this fest offers crawfish bread, crawfish pasta, crawfish pies, crawfish rice, crawfish jambalaya – infinite crawfish options, all of them good as hell. You'll also enjoy big carnival rides, regional arts and crafts, crawfish racing competitions, and more bands than you've seen, total, over the last five years. Four nights worth of "Cajun entertainment" builds up finally to the coronation of the Crawfish Queen. When we went last year, they were exhibiting a taxidermied two-headed albino cobra, but we're not sure it was real.

Natchitoches Meat Pie Fest and 10k Run

end of Oct., beginning of Sept., Natchitoches, LA [roughly 280 miles northwest of N.O.]

This one's a little far away, *but,* Oprah Winfrey once visited Natchitoches and declared it the "Best Little Town in the Whole USA." The festival takes place at the downtown riverbank along the Cane River Lake, with continuous live music, children's activities, a poker run, a "womanless" beauty pageant, a car show and a parade. Per the fest's theme, expect a meat pie making demonstration, a meat pie-making contest, and a meat pie-eating contest. Then there's a charity Fun Run, 'cause nothing's better after a load of meat pies than some running.

New Iberia Sugar Cane Fest

end of September, New Iberia, LA [130-odd miles west of N.O.], 337-369-9323; hisugar.org

Every little city in America hosts carnivals of rides and family fun, in some random field or gravel lot. But trust Louisiana's population to push any celebration to its max. This almost 70-year-old, free festival celebrating Louisiana's sugar growers (attendees are encouraged to "dress in farmer's attire") includes four days of giant rides and fair games, plus square-dancing presentations, a flower show, a boat parade, fireworks, a special Southern mass and authentic blessing of the crop, and of course, "sugar artistry." Numerous Cajun bands will be on hand to honor whomever is crowned **King and Queen Sucrose**. In terms of you getting the most dynamic, crazy taste of authentic Louisiana, Jazz Fest could never live up to this lil' celebration.

Ohr-O'Keefe Museum of Art

1596 Glen L. Swetman Dr. Biloxi, MS [hour and a half east of New Orleans], 228-374-5547; georgeohr.org

The mustachioed ceramicist **George Ohr** was known as the **Mad Potter of Biloxi**, and cultivated an eccentric persona during his life. His extraordinarily thin porcelain works were not particularly appreciated then, but he became well known around Biloxi as an oddball. Now, of course, he has a museum (and an annual mustache contest named for his Salvador Dali-esque facial hair). The pieces of Ohr's strangely attractive pottery that had been on display in Biloxi – some of his vases look like gloriously colorful crumpled paper bags, or deflated bullfrogs – were undamaged by the 2005 floods, and are now on display in the newly rebuilt, Gehry-designed museum.

Ponchatoula Strawberry Festival

three days at the beginning of April, 301 N 6th St Ponchatoula, LA [50 miles north of N.O.], 985-370-1889; lastrawberryfestival.com

This festival celebrating that sweet, lusty berry features rides, games (egg toss, sack race), bands, a cat judging contest, a Strawberry ball and coronation,

Daytrips

a baking contest, talent show, and a 10k "Strawberry Strut" competitive run. During almost no time does the live Louisiana music stop. Also, there are strawberries. Beware, though – the daiquiris are non-alcoholic.

Shearwater Pottery

102 Shearwater Drive #A Ocean Springs, MS [two hours east of New Orleans], 228-875-7320; walterandersonmuseum.org

For some reason, the tradition of art pottery is quite a thing in New Orleans and on the Gulf Coast. In Biloxi, along with the **George Ohr** collection and the **Walter Inglis Anderson** Museum – devoted to the Gulf Coast painter and potter – there is also the rebuilt Shearwater Pottery facility, where Anderson worked as a young man in the 20's. It's in a beautiful part of Ocean Springs near the water,

easily part of a Gulf Coast drive including the Ohr museum, and the earthenware pieces now being made there are indeed for sale.

Shrimp and Petroleum Festival

beginning of Sept., Morgan City LA [roughly 85 miles west of N.O.], Downtown Historic District, 985-385-0703; shrimp-petrofest.org

Just what is sounds like – a celebration of the products that keep the Gulf Coast economically afloat (after being recently, um, afloat in the bad way). There are rides, crafts, food, a 'Blessing of the Fleet' ceremony, and a water parade.

HOTELS / GUEST HOUSES

Living in New Orleans as we do, the authors of this book went into this section knowing just about nothing regarding places to stay for a night or two. Meaning we had to do a lot of research and make many calls in order to find nice places that aren't too expensive (and in the summer, you need a pool!). We found you some really good deals at fun places. You're welcome! We also included a couple fancier special bed and breakfasts. The prices of all New Orleans B&Bs fluctuate (except at Annabelle's House, below), so the end of each blurb states the absolute lowest price (always summer), a higher price (whenever the weather is nice, a.k.a. "festival season"), and each place's highest rates (during Mardi Gras or JazzFest). Most of these B&Bs provide wireless internet and continental breakfasts.

Hotel Monteleone

N FOX

1870 Banana Courtyard

French Quarter, 1422 N. Rampart St., 504-947-4475/800-842-4748; bananacourtyard.com

Each antique-appointed room has its own name in this 1870's house a half-block from the Quarter. The back relaxation area is tropical and the veranda hosts a hammock and a porch swing—stoop-sitting being a big New Orleans pasttime. $69 - $169.

AAE Bourbon

Uptown, 1660 Annunciation St., 504-644-2199; bourbon. aaeworldhotels.com

This hotel/hostel in the Garden District a block off of Magazine St. is perfectly situated for shopping and house-gawking, but pretty far from the French Quarter. The main mansion offers a party-hardy environment, and dorm beds start at $20 a night. Deluxe single rooms and other affordable private abodes house up to six guests.

A Creole Cottage

Marigny, 1827 Dauphine St., 504-948-4517; bbonline.com/la/creole

This circa 1810 Creole Cottage sits just one block from Bourbon Street and two blocks from Frenchmen. The one rental unit boasts a livingroom, bedroom, bathroom and a kitchen with a refrigerator for all the leftovers you will inevitably have after visiting our gluttonous restaurants. Price for up to two people: $70 - $115 - $130.

Annabelle's House Bed and Breakfast

Uptown, 1716 Milan Street; 504-250-1862; wix.com/randal1000/bed-and-breakfast

This 52 room Victorian mansion has three guestrooms. Continental breakfast includes fresh waffles. Their lowest rate ($99) is certainly not the lowest in town but their highest rate ($149) never fluctuates, even for Mardi Gras and other holidays.

Auld Sweet Olive Bed and Breakfast

Marigny, 2460 N. Rampart St., 877-470-5323; sweetolive.com

The former owner, an artist who worked in set design on many famous movies shot in New Orleans, also transformed the Sweet Olive into a work of live-in art. The website brags: "around each corner is another visual treat." Others now thoughtfully curate the former owner's works. $65 to $150.

Avenue Inn Bed and Breakfast

Uptown, 4125 St. Charles Ave., 1-800-490-8542; avenueinnbb.com

This 1891 Thomas Sully mansion is located in the shopping district that Magazine St. has become. It's steps from the street car line, and just off Lee Circle, home of The Circle Bar, one of the best (and smallest) clubs in the city (see *Parks and Other Family Stuff*).

Biscuit Palace

French Quarter, 730 Dumaine St., 504-525-9949; biscuitpalace.com

This under-advertised, funky guesthouse in the heart of the Quarter has very reasonable rates, and can't be beat for its geographic centrality. It's located inside a historic Creole mansion with a fading, ancient ad for Uneeda biscuits painted on the side – hence the name. Rooms are old-style New Orleans Storyville swank, and some have wrought-iron balconies looking out on Dumaine Street. You won't dig it if you're into W Hotel-style modernity. You'll love it if you think you're Tennessee Williams.

Bohemian Armadillo Guesthouse

Marigny, 735 Touro St., 512-297-9883; bohemianarmadillo.com

This great low-budge place asks for no minimum stay, has a hot tub, and also something called the "Bordello Room." Woo.

The Burgundy Bed and Breakfast

Bywater, 2513 Burgundy St., 800-970-2153; theburgundy.com

The Burgundy welcomes straight folks but it is definitely gay-ish. Meaning it is nice, and clean, with fascinating southern antiques, and though you can't smoke inside, outside you can sunbath nude–an option that really should appeal to anyone. $70 to $150.

Bywater Bed & Breakfast

Bywater, 1026 Clouet St., 504-944-8438; bywaterbnb.com

This rose-colored double shotgun offers, among the usual amenities, a library of books about New Orleans and a CD collection of Louisiana music, plus a sweet back patio with ceiling fan – perfect for reading whilst drinking. Rooms regularly $65-$75, or $125 during fall and winter festivals.

B&W Courtyards Bed and Breakfast

Marigny; 2425 Chartres St., 800-585-5731; bandwcourtyards.com

This award-winning restoration job consists of three 19th century buildings connected by courtyards, and features a Jacuzzi, massages if you need them, and continental breakfast (8:30 to 10am though? That's too early for adults partying in New Orleans!)

Coccinelle

Marigny, 2119 Decatur St., 504-943-9733; coccinellebandb.com

If you have a good job, Coccinelle offers rooms with private Jacuzzi tubs, all located in the former slave quarters of this Creole cottage with a second floor balcony overlooking a lush flagstone courtyard garden. Breakfast is sit-down gourmet. Dogs welcome. $125 to $175.

HOTELS

Creole Gardens and Guesthouse Bed & Breakfast

CBD, 1415 Prytania, St.,
866-596-8700; creolegardens.com

More like a hotel, with 24 guest rooms; large enough to host weddings. Located a block from the streetcar, and dog friendly with a dog park around the corner, Creole Gardens also provides a full southern breakfast. $69 to $129.

Creole Inn

Marigny, 2471 Dauphine St., 504-948-3230; www.creoleinn.com

Perfect for two couples, each double suites consist of two private bedrooms, rather than two beds in one room. No breakfast, but the beds are memory foam. Oooh. $49 (for five nights), $70 to $249 otherwise.

Crescent City Guest House

Marigny, 612 Marigny St., 877-281-2680; crescentcitygh.com

This pet-friendly guest house is sweetly located in the Marigny, and so close to the Quarter you can hear the calliope playing on the Mississippi from your hot tub (actually you can hear that thing's drunken hoot from almost anywhere in the city). Also features an enclosed sunbathing area, and gated off-street parking. $69 to $159.

Dauphine House

Marigny, 1830 Dauphine St.,
504-940-0943; dauphinehouse.com

Not the most bohemian of places, just your basic excellently restored two-story Pre-Civil War house with 12-foot ceilings and hardwood floors. Rooms each feature a private bath, small refrigerator, microwave, wireless internet, yadda yadda. Continental breakfast is left in your room. $65 to $125.

Dive Inn

Uptown, 4417 Dryades St.,
504-895-6555, 1-888-788-DIVE;
thediveinn.com

Located in a residential neighborhood, the Dive Inn is not especially convenient without a car or at least a bike, but they do provide some special, um, lifestyle amenities, namely a clothing-optional guest house. Dive Inn is quirky, homey, obviously quite relaxed, and centered on an indoor pool done up in watery tones with tropical plants and a stately mahogany-and-ivory island bar. Rooms are inexpensive, cozy and funky. No kids and no overt sexual themes; just good, old-fashioned, possibly naked fun.

Empress Hotel

Treme, 1317 Ursulines Ave.,
504-529-4100; empreshotel.com

The bare minimum (see the works of Bukowski). But all 36 rooms are just a very short (and sketchy) two-block walk from the French Quarter. This may be the place if you like unseemly adventure.

Fairchild House Bed and Breakfast
....
Uptown, 1518 Prytania St., 504-524-0154/800-256-8096; fairchildhouse.com

Courtyard for small weddings, with a Minister available if you get that drunk during your visit. Walking distance to the street car which will take you right to the Quarter. Propritor speaks Portuguese, English, French, Italian and Spanish. $79 - $149 - $199

Green House Inn
....
Lower Garden District, 1212 Magazine St., 504-525-1333/800-966-1303; thegreenhouseinn.com

Tropical gardens surround a heated saltwater swimming pool, huge jacuzzi hot tub. Clothing optional, so adults only. Three blocks from streetcar. $89 - $139 - $189

India House Hostel
....
Mid-City, 124 South Lopez St. [corner of Canal St.,] 504-821-1904; indiahousehostel.com

Unfortunately, only American students and foreign travelers are allowed to stay in this amazing big yellow house with its seasonal crawfish boils and "Indian Ocean" swimming pool. Communal rooms start at $17, while private 'Voodoo' and 'Bayou' cajun cabins,

which sleep two (communal bathrooms) are $45.00, as are private double rooms.

Joe & Flo Old Candlelight
....
Treme, 1129 N Robertson St., 504-581-6689

This hostel hasn't gotten too many rave reviews (they charge for toilet paper and "rent" towels), but should satisfy students and travelers on tight budgets, looking for just a roof over their head and a lock on their door. The staff makes up for the shortcomings in hospitality, though, and they offer cheap car service.

La Dauphine, Residence des Artistes
....
Marigny, 2316 Dauphine St., 504-948-2217; ladauphine.com

La Dauphine's **Alec Baldwin** Suite features the Louisiana cypress four-poster bed in which Alec made love to **Kelly Lynch** in the movie *Heaven's Prisoners*, filmed locally. The innkeepers speak Danish, Norwegian, Swedish, Spanish, English, French, and German, and yet state on their website, "We steer clear of the formal, pretentious crowd. We love to host nice, relaxed people who can 'go with the flow.'" Couples or singles only, no children or pets, and a three-night minimum stay is required.

Lions Inn
....
Marigny, 2517 Chartres St., 800-485-6846; lionsinn.com

Your basic pool, hot tub, and

breakfast joint, but with a communal piano, wedding facilities, "wine hour" every afternoon, and best of all: free use of in-house bicycles to pedal around town. Between the wine and the bikes, we fully endorse Lion's Inn. $50 to $165.

Lomothe House & The Frenchmen

Marigny, 417 Frenchman, 800-367-5858; lamothehouse.com

This architectural wonder built in 1839 now has a heated jacuzzi and pool and serves continental breakfast. 24-hour front desk. $99 to $299

Lookout Inn

Bywater, 833 Poland Ave., 888-947-8188; lookoutneworleans.com

Located by the Naval Annex, Lookout Inn is named for its tower, where the Navy/ladyboys would keep lookout on the Mississippi during WWII. Upon request, the staff will arrange yoga instruction, oyster and shrimp parties, wine tastings and other good times. Lookout also has an awesome little saltwater pool and Jacuzzi. Though you're deep in the neighborhood (you will surely be the only tourist), it's a *great* spot for killer restaurants (**The Joint** bbq, **Jack Dempsey's** fried seafood) and dive bars like **B.J.'s** and the inimitable **Vaughan's** (free food and live music Thursdays,

holidays, and intermittently in between). Rooms start at $59.

Marquette House Hostel

Uptown, 2249 Carondelet St., 504-523-3014; neworleansinternationalhostel.com

A bare-bones, possibly smelly lil' hostel with $25 beds. But it has a bar, and is near other bars such as **Igor's**, and after a bloody mary or two, it's fun to stumble out into the street and onto the streetcar and relax on a long slow ride through half of the city.

Marigny Manor House

Marigny, 2125 N. Rampart St., 504-943-7826; marignymanorhouse.com

An affordable, quaint, restored 1840's Greek revival house located super close to Frenchmen St.'s music clubs and restaurants (as well as **Gene's Po-Boys and Daiquiris**, the bright pink building on Elysian Fields and St. Claude; highly recommended).

New Orleans Guest House

Treme, 1118 Ursulines St., 800-562-1177; neworleans.com/nogh

This salacious pink building on the Rampart St. side of the French Quarter is an 1848 gable-sided Creole cottage, its insides as funky as its outside. Rooms start at $79.

The Lookout Inn in a far back quiet corner of Bywater, among a paradise of dive bars and down-home restaurants.

Parkview Marigny Bed and Breakfast

Marigny; 726 Frenchmen St., 877-645-8617; neworleansbb.com

135-year-old Creole townhouse, the owner of which is a great breakfast cook. Laundry on site. $125 to $160.

Rathbone Inn

Mid-City, 1244 Esplanade Ave., 504-309-4479; rathbonemansions.com

Two mansions across the street from one another on gorgeous Esplanade Ave. bordering the French Quarter. One mansion features a pool and Jacuzzi, the other a lush courtyard for chillin'. Cheapest rooms are $59 during summer, while the most expensive during Mardi Gras cost $250 for a courtyard suite with kitchenette and three beds (sleeps six).

The Red Door at Creole Inn

Marigny, 2471 Dauphine St., 813-326-0897; creoleinn.com

In this unassuming little Marigny cottage, the double suites all have 2 private bedrooms, rather than just one room with two beds like a hotel. Red Door enforces a "quiet hour" after 9:30, but if you want, the owners can "take your party on the road in a 30 passenger cruiser" (check *partyonwheelsusa. com* for prices). No breakfast. Rooms start at $59.

Royal Barracks Guest House

French Quarter, 717 Barracks St., 504-529-7269: rbgh.com

The bunk room, garden room, gothic room and peacock room with ten-foot chandalier were each designed by a different local artist. The pool is temporarily

HOTELS

out of service but the courtyard wet bar is open. $69 - $149 - $299

Schiro's Balcony Guest House Bed and Breakfast
....
Marigny, 2483 Royal St., 800-395-2124; balconyguesthouse.com

You couldn't ask for a better locale than this b&b above Schiro's grocery, laundry and restaurant, which serves New Orleans style breakfast, lunch and dinner, along with a short menu of Indian dishes. Tucked into the neighborhood, its also right smack in the middle of two coffeeshops, a bookstore, half-a-dozen great nighttime hangouts (some with live music), and other plusses. So much entertainment, you may forget about Frenchmen St. and The Quarter just a few blocks away. $79 during the summer, and $129 during peak season.

St. Peter House
French Quarter, 1005 Saint Peter St., 504-524-9232/800-535-7815
Aside from its nice price, this tropical brick courtyard with broad iron-lace balconies is exactly what one would expect of a French Quarter hotel. Continental breakfast included. $59 - $79 - $199

St. Vincent (Hotel and Hostel)
....
Uptown, 1507 Magazine St., 504-302-9606; stvguesthouse.com

This 70-room hotel boasts an on-site restaurant, bike rental (all New Orleans hotels and b&b should loan bikes to their clientele!), private rooms, plus male, female and co-ed dormitories with 3 to 6 beds. Dorms run from $20 to $45, while hotel rooms hover around $69 all year.

N.O. MOMENT:

ROYAL STREET INN / R BAR
AND ITS ILLUSTRIOUS ROCKSTAR OWNER,
GREG DULLI

Marigny, 1431 Royal St., 504-948-7499; royalstreetinn.com

More of a "bed and beverage," owing to the R Bar downstairs–
a place essential to any New Orleans visit anyway, with its
intermittent free shrimp and crawfish boils, and DJ's almost
nightly spinning everything from old New Orleans R&B, garage
rock, to weird ancient country, to whatever rock is cool in
Brooklyn. On Monday nights, $10 will get you a shot, a beer, and
a haircut by a semi-professional stylist. R Bar is now owned in
part by former **Afghan Whigs** frontman and current **Twilight
Singer** and **Gutter Twin**, **Greg Dulli**. Upstairs the rooms are

decorated for maximum "sleazy luxury." One room was formerly
named the **Bukowski** Suite, for the author who stayed there and
etched 'Hank Was Here' in the cement outside the bar door. The
rooms are much nicer now.

GETTING AROUND: BIKES AND PUBLIC TRANSPORTATION

New Orleans' public transportation is not necessarily to be relied upon. A nicer way to put this would be: rent a bike. Even on a beach cruiser, you can pedal from one end of the city's heart to the other "far" end, in an hour. There is no better way to see the city, especially the French Quarter, so long as you know when not to pedal where (we've sprinkled these tips throughout). Choose to drive, and parking can be nightmarish. Rely only on your feet, and risk missing chunks of the Quarter. On a bike you'll cover the most ground, and see the most sights. Plus, the city is almost entirely flat.

However, one way in which New Orleans is not, in fact, a charming Stateside slice of Europe is that there are very few bike paths anywhere. Nor are there many places to rent bikes. The city could really help cure its own poverty, obesity, and bad roads by encouraging bicycle use, but... anyway.

Nolacycle.com *provides great information on New Orleans' bike culture (not sports-oriented 'bike culture,' more like bikes with cup-holders on the handlebars and other whimsical decorations, like fake flowers) with listings of local bohemian bicycle events, and downloadable New Orleans biking maps. The following local bike shops are also fighting the good two-wheeled fight – meaning they'll rent you a bike:*

ZS

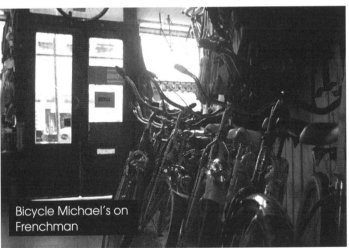

Bicycle Michael's on Frenchman

9th Ward Bike Tours

....

634 Elysian Fields Ave., 504-909-9959; ninthwardrebirthbiketours.com

This four-hour bike tour takes you past Bywater into the formerly devisated Lower 9th Ward. On comfortable cruiser-style bicycles, the tour aims to introduce riders to local survivors, and help them comprehend the struggle of this unique community. Ronald Lewis of House of Dance and Feathers will regale you with stories of social clubs, second line parades and Mardi Gras Indians. After lunch at a neighborhood po-boy shop, swing by Fats Domino's house and hear tales of legendary R&B stars, then sit upon a floodwall overlooking Bayou Bienvenu to learn about the importance of Louisiana wetlands. A lot of beauty to be seen via this tour, and a great way to support the community. $55 tours Mon. – Sat.

Bicycle Michael's

Marigny, 622 Frenchmen St.; 504-945-9505; bicyclemichaels.com

As far as legitimate professional (but still a tad funky) bike shops go, Michael's has a monopoly over the Marigny/Bywater. They're kinda pricey on some things, and sometimes the staff's kind of gruff, but they do set aside a gate outside of their shop for bands to post fliers. Bike rental is $25 a day.

The Bike Shop

Uptown, 4711 Freret St., 265-8071

features new and used bicycles for adults and children. They also repair, buy bikes and have records for sale. Pick up all your bike accessories including baskets, bells, racks, helmets and more! Featuring new Sun brand bikes.

Confederacy of Cruisers Bike Tours

Marigny; 634 Elysian Fields; 400-5468; confederacyofcruisers.com

This Marigny company offers a Creole New Orleans Bicycle Tours, a History of Drinking in New Orleans Bike Tour, and a New Orleans Culinary Bike Tour, among other experiences.

Gerken's Bike Shop

Bywater, 2703 Saint Claude Ave., 504-373-6924

A down-home, cheap bike shop in a funky area on the railroad tracks (right by the Green Project, an architectural salvage spot that's a junk collector's dream). Gerken's caters to the neighborhood boho bike crowd. They buy a lot of their parts from New Orleans' charity bike project, Plan B, but they'll fix stuff for you. Gerken's doesn't directly rent bikes, but call them and they'll figure something out for you.

Mike the Bike Guy

Uptown, 4411 Magazine St; 504-899-1344; mikethebikeguy.com

This particular Mike worked fixing bikes for others for 20 years before opening his own place. Bikes rent for $30 a day, $120 for a week, but once one of the bikes has been used for a week, Mike sells them for around $130.

Plan B: New Orleans Community Bike Project

Marigny, 511 Marigny St., 504-944-0366; bikeproject.org

The mission of Plan B on the corner of Marigny and Decatur Streets is to "rescue useful bikes and parts from the trash and reuse them to counter the extreme wastefulness of industrialized nations." They won't fix your bike for you, but rather, will provide free workspace, tools and advice, plus used and new parts for small donations. For roughly $35 to $75 (the cost of a regular three-day bike rental elsewhere) you can build your own Plan B bike alongside smart, strange, fun New Orleanians, ride the bike all through Mardi Gras or Jazz Fest, then donate it back to Plan B. Weird hours, though: Monday: 2-6pm, Tuesday, 2-6pm (reserved for ladies and transgendered people), Thursday: 4-8pm Saturday: 2-6pm.

Laid-back Bike Tours

Mid-City, 1815 Elysian Fields Ave., 504-400-5468; confederacyofcruisers.com

Comfortable beach cruisers rent for $25 a day, including free delivery and pickup, plus helmet, lock and basket. The shop is right on Bayou St. John, an amazing bike route with almost no car traffic. Pedal around the water or through Mid-City's truly gorgeous residential streets. Confederacy also gives great three-hour, eight-mile tours that expose tourists to non-French Quarter neighborhoods, and provide insight into neighborhood architecture, Mardi Gras Indians, and New Orleans R&B music.

R.U.B.A.R.B

Bywater, 2239 Piety St.; rubarbike.org

An acronym for *rusted up beyond all recognition bikes,* this is another community bike shop where you can learn to build or repair a bike, obtain a bike through work trade or a suggested donation of $40-$75, send your child on a field-trip, or even just volunteer. Unlike Plan B, Rubarb also offers some rentals during major New Orleans holidays, with all donations going back into the shop to purchase tools as well as art supplies (because your bike has to costume on Mardi Gras too!) Mon 10am-2pm, Wed 3:30-6pm, Sat 1-6pm.

Kayak-iti-Yat

985-778-5034 or 512-964-9499; kayakitiyat.com

Kayak right up the middle of a community filled with little neighborhood parks, great food, fun bars and sometimes festivals or Mardi Gras Indians.

PUBLIC TRANSPORTATION

City buses (RTA)

504-248-3900; norta.com

After flying into the Lil Wayne International Airport, you can take the $1.25 city bus into town, rather than wasting $30 on a cab ($30 is ten drinks in many New Orleans bars!) Once you're in town, though, you'd only choose a bus over bike for A/C, or to dodge rain, or when shopping on Magazine St., where they run straight and efficiently up and down miles of shops and cafes. Otherwise, our city busses are mostly only good for meeting interesting local characters, which you will indeed. (From the airport, you can also get the Airport Shuttle for about $15, which will drop you at any hotel or guest house).

Greyhound Buses

CBD, 1001 Loyola Ave;
504-524-7571; greyhound.com

When needing to flee New Orleans at a moment's notice, Greyhound provide spectacular and economic getaways for lawless fugitives, and fauxbeauxs utilizing mom's gold card for a break from train-hopping.

Mule Buggies

French Quarter, 504-944-0366

Especially during the hell-hot summer, those poor animals don't want to drag you around the French Quarter. All summer the poor things sweat, their tongues twisting and writhing trying to spit that bit out of their mouths. No matter how good the mules are supposedly treated, they'd be much happier if you just rode a bike and let them be.

The Streetcar

504-248-3900

Same as our city busses: $1.25, every fifteen minutes, though you can often out-walk the streetcar to your destination. But of course that's not the point; all visitors should ride the streetcar once. Especially if one of the cooler drivers lets you sneak your daiquiri onboard, it's great to ride slow and long through the CBD, staring out the window at all the poor suckers working, before snaking around Lee Circle and into the big trees and mansions of Uptown, where the vast yards look empty without servants tending to the flower beds and such. The streetcar ain't meant for reaching important destinations on time, but then, you could realistically share a streetcar with a brass band practicing on their way to a gig. Cars run 5am to roughly 2am.

Taxis

United Cab, 504-522-9771;
unitedcabs.com

Unless you're on Frenchmen Street, Esplanade, Decatur, or Canal, where you can usually flag one down, you'll need to phone for a cab. United is the local favorite.

HELPFUL NEW ORLEANS PUBLICATIONS AND WEBSITES

Here are informative and fun websites you can check for New Orleans entertainment and culture news, and also printed publications you can pick up while you're in town.

LOCAL PUBLICATIONS

AntiGravity

antigravitymagazine.com

If you like this guidebook, you'll probably dig Antigravity. AG a street-level view of the NOLA music scene; a kind of alternate musical universe with more info on punk, metal, indy and underground sounds than you're likely to find in the older, more established publications.

Gambit Weekly

bestofneworleans.com

This is New Orleans' only alternative weekly and is usually a great source for music and arts listings.One of the contributors to this book, **Alison Fensterstock**, held down their music coverage between 2006 and 2009, and Michael is a frequent freelancer. *Gambit* focuses on left-of-center politics and A&E coverage, and does its best to give equal space to both traditional and edgy happenings in the print publication and the blog site, *blogofneworleans.com*.

OffBeat

offbeat.com

This over 20-year-old music magazine doesn't always have its ear to New Orleans' streets, but *OffBeat* is the authority on all things traditional. They review almost every Louisiana CD released, and at times can take you deeper into Louisiana roots music than any other local publication. This book's co-author, Michael Patrick Welch, pioneered a monthly "alternative music" column for them that lasted between 2003 and 2005.

The Times-Picayune

nola.com

Besides having a truly great name, the *Times-Picayune* newspaper is a fairly legit, Pulitzer-winning daily. The weekly Lagniappe pullout, which comes out on Fridays, features their (admittedly middle-of-the-road) arts, music and culture picks for the week ahead. This is where you'll now find **Alison Fensterstock**.

Where Y'at?

whereyat.com

Where Y'at? magazine is a slim little tabloid full of ads, bar guides, ads, some music coverage, and some ads. Very good entertainment for when you're at a bar and your date goes to use the bathroom and is there a long time.

NEW ORLEANS WEBSITES

BestofNewOrleans.com

The *Gambit's* website with news, reviews and listings; an online version of the paper. *Blogofneworleans.com* is The Gambit's blog site, with extended interviews from the print version, news bits and bytes, plus more colloquial tidbits on local goings-on.

Defendneworleans.com

Maker of now-iconic shirts and throwers of parties, their site features blogs and videos of hipster antics, such as, what happens when a bounce rapper plays a debutante party.

Goner-records.com

The New Orleans section of its lively message board is great for garage and punk show listings and entertaining scene gossip.

Homeofthegroove.com

An exhaustively informative music blog that digs deep into New Orleans R&B and rock n'roll history.

Humidcity.com

A smart, snarky blog of news-driven commentary and colorful musings that gives great context for this strange city and its goings-on.

Nola.com

The Times-Picayune's site – realtime breaking news and liveblog coverage of crimes and music festivals.

Nolafugees.com

Sarcastic but often informative news. They've self-published a few books of essays that dealt primarily with life after the 2005 flood.

Noladefender.com

Community journalism, entertainment listings and free mixtapes by famous locals.

Noladiy.com

Incredibly thorough listings for all punk, metal and otherwise underground shows, including house parties and the like.

Offbeat.com

Music news, reviews and listings. Editor **Alex Rawls'** *Pop Life* blog extends the magazine's fairly Catholic coverage into more general musings on the music world, and music news that paints a little more well-rounded picture of the city.

Wwoz.org

Streaming realtime audio from the station, plus DJ blogs, playlists and community news.

S.O.S.: HELP POST-KATRINA NEW ORLEANS!

Five years after Katrina, most of New Orleans is still in dire need (honestly, a lot of New Orleans' infrastructure was screwy enough to need professional help before the storm, but now...man). The following groups have specifically helped New Orleans and its musicians in one form or another, and all of them will gladly accept your donations:

Sweet Home New Orleans

....

sweethomeneworleans.org

One-stop shopping for musicians in need, Sweet Home's comprehensive caseworker system hooks up musicians with housing, legal, medical and cash grant assistance.

New Orleans Musicians' Clinic

....

neworleansmusiciansclinic.org

This venerable sliding scale clinic gives uninsured musicians access to **LSU Healthcare Network** physicians.

Make It Right Foundation

makeitrightnola.org

Brad Pitt's cause célèbre builds green housing in the areas most ravaged by the flood. Said houses are all odd but cool twists on traditional New Orleans architecture. Drive down to the Lower Nine and check 'em out.

Habitat for Humanity

habitat-nola.org

Locally, this national organization dedicated a block of houses – the **Musicians' Village**, in the Upper Ninth Ward – for New Orleans musicians who qualified for their program.

Hands On New Orleans

handsonneworleans.org

This volunteer aggregator partners eager volunteers with needy causes in New Orleans. Since Katrina, they've mobilized over 15,000 volunteers.

One of actor Brad Pitt's post-Katrina 9th Ward housing and art projects. Pitt is a cool person who's helped New Orleans a lot.

ABOUT THE AUTHORS:

Michael Patrick Welch is the author of the memoir *Commonplace* (*Screw Music Forever Press*), *Y'all's Problem* (*Dirty Coast*) and the New Orleans novel *The Donkey Show* (*Equator Books*). He has freelanced for *Gambit Weekly* for many years, served as a staff writer/editorial assistant at the *St Petersburg Times* and penned a column in New Orleans' oldest music magazine, *OffBeat*. His freelance work has also appeared in *Newsweek*, *Spin*, and several Village Voice publications. Welch also teaches a music writing class for public school kids (*myspace.com/mrmichaelsclass*) and acts as bandleader for electro-rock-n-R&B band, The White Bitch. Email him at michaelpatrickwelch@gmail.com

Alison Fensterstock served as *Gambit Weekly*'s music writer from 2006-9, before moving on to write about music for *The Times-Picayune*. She is the winner of 4 New Orleans Press Club awards for features writing and or her Gambit music column. Her work has appeared in *Paste*, *MOJO*, the *Oxford American*, *Vibe*, *Q* and *Spin.com*. Her Gambit story "Sissy trut," about the phenomenon of gay bounce rappers in New Orleans, received an honorable mention in the 2009 edition of Da Capo's Best Music Writing. Recently, she served as the researcher for the *Where They At?* multimedia museum exhibit about the history of New Orleans bounce" music.

Jack Smith is an editorial and fine art portrait photographer, curator of the Canary Gallery on Julia Street, and also plays drums in the revered New Orleans rock band, Rotary Downs. He has recently been the official photographer of the New Orleans Jazz and Heritage Festival, and is an instructor of photography at the New Orleans Academy of Fine Art. His work has appeared in *Rolling Stone* and *Filter*.

Jonathan Traviesa has been photographing in New Orleans since 1997. In 2009, UNO Press published a monograph of his portrait work, "*Portraits: Photographs in New Orleans, 1998-2009.*" Concurrent to the book release, the Ogden Museum of Southern Art exhibited a solo show of his work from this series. His prints are collected privately around the United States and publicly in New Orleans by the Ogden and the New Orleans Museum of Art. Traviesa is a founding member of The Front, a contemporary art gallery in New Orleans, and his editorial work has been published in news and fashion magazines around the world. He also owns the world's most memorable hair.

INDEX

NOTE: *Because of our focus on music, we decided to list people's names not how you would read them from the phone book (ie. Scurvics, Ratty) but instead as you would read them on a flier stapled to a light post (ie. Ratty Scurvics). Names in* **bold (and p.) correspond to photographs.**